# THE ARAB
# CONQUESTS

# THE LANDMARK LIBRARY

*Chapters in the History of Civilization*

The Landmark Library is a record of the achievements of humankind
from the late Stone Age to the present day. Each volume in the series
is devoted to a crucial theme in the history of civilization, and offers
a concise and authoritative text accompanied by a generous
complement of images. Contributing authors to the Landmark
Library are chosen for their ability to combine
scholarship with a flair for communicating their
specialist knowledge to a wider,
non-specialist readership.

# THE ARAB
# CONQUESTS

## THE SPREAD OF
## ISLAM AND THE
## FIRST CALIPHATES

JUSTIN MAROZZI

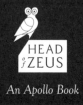

HEAD
of ZEUS

An Apollo Book

*To Julia and Clem,
who conquered me*

An Apollo book
First published in the UK in 2021
by Head of Zeus Ltd

3 5 7 9 10 8 6 4 2

A CIP catalogue record for this book is available
from the British Library.

ISBN (HB) 9781838933401
ISBN (E) 9781838933418

Designed by Isambard Thomas at Corvo
Maps by Jamie Whyte
Colour separation by DawkinsColour
Printed in Spain by Graficas Estella

Head of Zeus Ltd
First Floor East
5–8 Hardwick Street
London EC1R 4RG

WWW.HEADOFZEUS.COM

*previous pages*
'A pearl set in emeralds'. Moorish arches in the
Court of the Lions in the Alhambra de Granada,
the most famous example of Islamic architecture
in Andalusia, Muslim Al Andalus.

North
Sea

FRANKS

AVARS

Bay
of
Biscay

LOMBARDS

Danube

Ravenna

Black

VISIGOTHS

Rome

BYZANTINE

Constantinop

Toledo

Anat

Mediter

Ephesus

Cordoba

Carthage

Tangiers

BYZACENA

MAURETANIA

AFRICA PROCONSULARIS

Tripoli

Barqa

Alexandria

CYRENAICA

Babylon
Fortress

N

Nile

THE     WORLD
ON  THE  EVE  OF  THE
ARAB  CONQUESTS
AD   630

0          200          400          600

Miles

North
Sea

FRANKS

Bay
of
Biscay

LOMBARDS

VISIGOTHS

Rome

Danube

AVARS

Constantinople

Bla

E M

Mediterranean Sea

BYZANTINE

Sbeitla
(647)

Battle of
the Masts
(655)

Tripoli

Barqa

Alexandria
(642)

Sabratah

(643)

Heliopo
(640)

(642)

Aswar

Nile

(643)

M A K

A L O

# A R A B
## C O N Q U E S T S
### A D   6 3 4 – 6 6 1

0        200        400        600

Miles

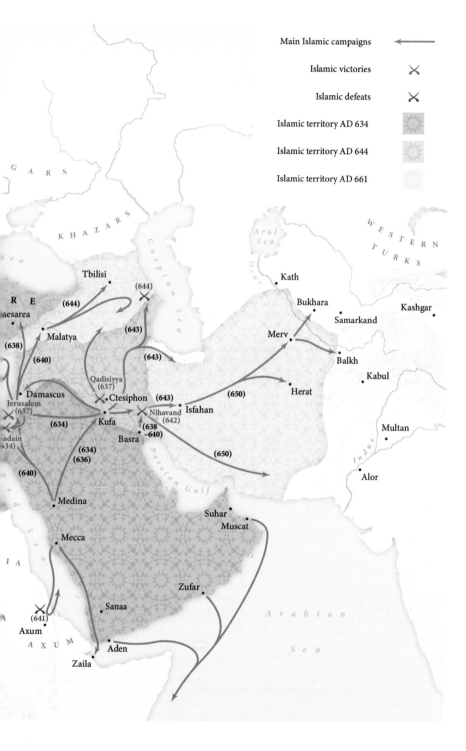

Main Islamic campaigns

Islamic victories

Islamic defeats

Islamic territory AD 634

Islamic territory AD 644

Islamic territory AD 661

G A R S

KHAZARS

Aral Sea

W E S T E R N

T U R K S

Tbilisi

(644)

Caspian Sea

Kath

Bukhara

Kashgar

R    E

aesarea

(644)

(643)

Samarkand

Malatya

Merv

(638)

(643)

Balkh

(640)

(643)

Kabul

Qadisiyya
(637)

Herat

Damascus

Ctesiphon

(643)

(650)

Jerusalem
(637)

Kufa

Nihavand
(642)

Isfahan

adain
34)

(634)

(638
-640)

Basra

Multan

(640)

(634)
(636)

(650)

Medina

Alor

Suhar

Muscat

Mecca

Indus

Zufar

A r a b i a n

I A

Sanaa

Axum

(641)

S e a

A X U M

Aden

Zaila

North
Sea

*Bay
of
Biscay*

CAROLINGIAN

**Tours
732** ✖

EMPIRE

*Danube*

AQUITAINE

AVAR

KHAGANATE

Black

✖
**Narbonne
719-20**

LOMBARDS

**Constantinople** •

A N D A L U S

BYZANTINE E

Toledo •

Cordoba •

*Mediterranean*

S

✖ **Carthage
698**

**Tangiers
708** ✖

Sbeitla •

• Qairouan

*Sea*

L

A Tripoli •

M

• Barqa

Alexandria

I

Misr al Fustat •

C

Babyl

• Ghadames

E G Y P

F A Z Z A N

Aswan

*Nile*

M A K

Dongola •

# T H E     I S L A M I C
E M P I R E
A D   7 5 0

A L O

0          200          400          600

Miles

# Introduction

*It goes something like this.*

A thousand warriors on a thousand horses gallop full tilt across a shimmering horizon. Rolling thunder and a sandstorm stirred up by four thousand hooves mingle with the martial roars of the horsemen. On and on ride the cavalry in a God-given frenzy of conquest. Menace hangs in the air. Date palms wilt in the heat. Now they descend on a ragged, sun-ravaged settlement. Panic shoots through the beleaguered inhabitants, too slow to react, too weak to resist these invading aristocrats of the desert. Sheep and goats bleat, camels bellow in distress. Cries of terror and flashing steel. Women and children scream. Swords whirl, heads roll and lifeless bodies slump to the ground. Blood drains into the desert. There is the briefest of pauses. A few moments to pillage anything of value before the warriors remount their sleek steeds and ride on, a handful of howling women added to their ranks. New triumphs await the Arabian horsemen, and their sons and grandsons, across the farthest horizons on distant continents. In a few generations they will have turned the world upside down.

This childish mise en scène, a clumsy composite of Quran and *Boys' Own*, is how I have always pictured the Arab Conquests. Yet the truth is there is no way of knowing what they were *really* like. For all the stirring chronicles and accounts, there are virtually no detailed descriptions of battlefield encounters and precious little visual or archaeological evidence to show us what a seventh-century Arab fighter and his equipment actually looked like. The historian, scouring for evidence and vanishingly elusive first-hand accounts, must make do with partial and patchy records, after-the-event history written much later both by the victors, puffed up with pride, and the stricken losers, who have fallen into the apocalypse. There is only so much to go on when peering into the seventh and eighth centuries.

Yet perhaps that lurid, blood-spattered picture is less far-fetched than we might think. It is not so far removed, after all, from the ancient Bedouin poetry that celebrated the time-honoured desert raids on enemy tribes with great gusto. In a typical example of the genre, the poet Amir ibn al Tufayl, a contemporary of the Prophet Mohammed, recalled a lightning attack on his enemies:

> We came upon them at dawn with our tall steeds,
> > lean and sinewy and spears whose steel was
> > as burning flame…
> We came upon their host in the morning,
> > and they were like a flock of sheep on whom
> > falls the ravening wolf…
> We fell on them with white steel ground to keenness:
> > we cut them to pieces until they were destroyed;
> And we carried off their women on the saddles behind us,
> > with their cheeks bleeding, torn in anguish by their nails.[1]

If we have to exercise our imaginations and reconstruct some scenes to picture what really happened, then that is only to be expected when dealing with events that happened in far-off places almost 1,400 years ago. And besides, lest we become too gloomy about the prospects of establishing how the conquests unfolded with some level of confidence, there is much that does not depend on our imaginative powers, much that is absolutely beyond question.

We know, for example, that the Arab Conquests followed immediately after the Prophet Mohammed's death in 632. By this time, against all the odds, he had managed to unite the disparate, forever-feuding tribes of Arabia at the point of his sword. We know, too, that these great conquests lasted until 750, by which time several generations of marauding Arab armies had carved out an Islamic empire which, in terms of size and population, rivalled that of Rome at its zenith, extending from the shores of

*overleaf* Bedouin tribesmen and their camel caravan travelling in Wadi Rum, Jordan. Surging out of the Arabian deserts to the south, their warrior ancestors spearheaded the Arab Conquests of the seventh and eighth centuries.

the Atlantic and the Iberian Peninsula in the west to the snow-bound mountain passes of Central Asia and the borders of China in the east. In the process, they had completely crushed one great empire and hollowed out another.

Ascendant for more than 400 years across Iran, Iraq, swathes of Central Asia, Anatolia and the Caucasus, the Sasanian Empire of Persia breathed its last under the Arab onslaught. In 651, powerless to repel rampant Arab forces swarming across his kingdom, unable to raise an army to protect his disintegrating empire, Yazdgird III was reduced to ignominious flight. After a valiant last stand near the ancient city of Merv, he abandoned his horse with its golden saddle, his mace and his sword in its golden sheath and took refuge on a pile of straw in a watermill. Here the man who revelled in the ancient title of Shahanshah, King of Kings, was treacherously betrayed and fatally stabbed by the miller. 'This is the way of the deceitful world,' wrote the peerless Persian poet Ferdowsi in his epic *Shahnameh* (*Book of Kings*), 'raising a man up and casting him down. When fortune was with him, his throne was in the heavens, and now a mill was his lot; the world's favours are many, but they are exceeded by its poison.'[2] It was the end of the Sasanian dynasty and the demise of Iran's last pre-Islamic empire. The country would never be the same again.

Further to the west, the Arabs had also ridden roughshod over vast tracts of the Byzantine Empire, seizing control of Egypt, its breadbasket, and North Africa, together with the fabled Holy Land in Syria and Palestine, while the God-fearing residents of Constantinople had trembled at the appearance of successive Arab armies – and even a fleet – before the city's mighty walls.

We know, in other words, that the Arab Conquests of the seventh and eighth centuries represented one of the greatest feats of arms in history and utterly changed the world – both as

An Arab warrior mounted on his camel, as depicted in the spectacularly illustrated thirteenth-century manuscript *Al Maqamat* by the poet and scholar Al Hariri. The conquerors travelled fast and light, living off the land and eschewing ponderous supply caravans.

أوَّزتْهُ فغادَرَنا بعدَ أنْ وَحِدَتْ عِطْفَهُ وزالَ لَنا

أُنسُهُ كادَتْ غابَ صدرُهُ أوْ لَيلُ أوَّلُ بَدْرُه

## المقامة التاسعة عشرة

روى الحارثُ بنُ هِمامٍ قالَ أخَذَ العِراقُ دارَ العُمرِ

لِلأَخلاقِ أنواءُ العَيشِ وتَجدَّدَ الرُّكّابُ بِنَصِيبِينَ

وبِهَفْنَةِ أهلِهَا المَحصِبينَ أُقدِمُ مُهرِيًا واعْتَقَلْتُ سُمْهَرِيًا

contemporaries understood it then and as we, with the benefit of fourteen centuries of hindsight, know it today.

If a great deal of confusion and uncertainty still hangs over the Arab Conquests today – how exactly did these relatively few warriors overthrow two great empires so swiftly, what were their motivations, precisely who among the conquered people threw in their lot with the all-conquering Arabs? – this is as nothing when compared to the utter shock and incomprehension experienced by those Christians at the time who were the first to succumb to Arab steel.

For centuries the Byzantines had faced off against their eastern neighbours the Persians, whom they rightly considered their principal adversary. They might not have liked each other but both sides were nothing if not familiar with each other. For an entire generation, from 602 to 628, the two ancient enemies had battered each other virtually to a standstill in the devastating Byzantine–Sasanian War. In 614 Jerusalem fell to the Persians after a brief siege. Then, in 637, only five years after the death of the Prophet Mohammed and with Byzantine power restored, the distraught Patriarch Sophronius of Jerusalem found himself surrendering the keys of the Holy City not to another general from the Persian Empire, which was by then close to terminal collapse, but to the camel-mounted Arab caliph Umar, leader of an entirely new, completely unknown and radically militant faith from the Arabian desert. It was an annihilating moment for Sophronius. During his Christmas Eve sermon of 634 he had warned his flock of 'the slime of the godless Saracens', who were perpetrating 'every diabolical savagery' across the Holy Land. He considered the fall of Jerusalem 'the abomination of desolation', as foretold by the prophet Daniel, and died soon afterwards of a broken heart.[3] Yet for the Christians, Zoroastrians, Jews, Manichaeans, Mandaeans, pagans, Buddhists and Hindus of the Middle East, North Africa, Central Asia and the Indian subcontinent in the seventh and eighth centuries, this was merely one of the first explosions of the firestorm that was to rage across the world.

Our story does not end with the conquests. Staring back through the ages at that momentous period from 632 until 750, we can see that it set the stage for a no less remarkable phenomenon – a cultural flowering in which the new-born Islamic world became the greatest, most sophisticated civilization on earth. Spiritually superior from its own perspective, it was militarily, economically and culturally pre-eminent from that of everyone else. Had it not been for the continent-spanning Arab Conquests, there would have been no Islamic Empire to champion and incubate the extraordinary intellectual advances in science, medicine, mathematics, astronomy, cartography, calligraphy, history, geography, law, music, theology, jurisprudence and philosophy that illuminated the world for centuries to come. Under the Abbasids, who in 750 replaced the Umayyads as leaders of the Islamic world from their new capital of Baghdad, 'Arab Muslims now studied astronomy, alchemy, medicine and mathematics with such success that, during the ninth and tenth centuries, more scientific discoveries had been achieved in the Abbasid Empire than in any previous period of history'.[4] Little wonder that this period has been likened to Greece's Golden Age of the fifth century BC.

If those achievements look distinctly historical and irrelevant to daily life today, there is another more suited to the here and now, audible every day on the streets of Algiers, Baghdad, Beirut, Cairo, Damascus, Doha, Dubai, Mecca, Muscat, Rabat, Riyadh, Sanaa, Tripoli, Tunis and far beyond. 'The Arab tongue is the widest-ranging of tongues, and the most copious in vocabulary,' wrote the eighth-century scholar Al Shafi. 'We are aware of no person who can encompass a complete knowledge of it, unless that person be a prophet.'[5] That is surely true, and no man or woman may ever completely master this maddeningly rich and complex language, but without the conquests Arabic would never have become the lingua franca of 450 million Arabs from Morocco to Oman, a distance of 4,000 miles. While political unity has proved dispiritingly elusive for Arabs over many centuries, the common tongue of classical Arabic – *arabiyyah* – has become, with Islam, the immovable bedrock of their cultural unity.

While scholarship and language are two lasting legacies of those early conquests, then faith is arguably the third and most influential. '*Allahu akbar! Allahu akbar!*' the minarets sing – in Arabic – from one end of the *Dar al Islam*, the Muslim world, to the other. 'God is greatest! God is greatest!' Five times a day, the famous call to prayer sounds far and wide beyond the Arabic-speaking countries of the Middle East, from Bradford to Marseille, Kabul to Khartoum and Kuala Lumpur, Sarajevo to Samarkand, Jaipur to Jakarta. It unites the entire *ummah*, or Muslim community, by calling to prayer those who have made the submission (*Islam* in Arabic) to the one true God. This is a faith that governs all aspects of life from cradle to grave and counts 1.8 billion men, women and children, around a quarter of the world's population, among its adherents. The foundation of an obscure faith in the Arabian desert was one thing. Its diffusion far and wide by sword-wielding, Quran-bearing Arabian warriors was quite another. Had it not been for these men, it is quite possible that Islam might never have survived or would have remained a minor cult limited to the sun-tormented cities and burning wilderness of the peninsula. Had it not been for their astonishingly audacious and triumphant campaigns, it is surely doubtful that Islam would have become a global faith then and the world's fastest-growing religion today.

During the age of the great conquests, surging north from the Arabian Peninsula, the Arabs came to the world. In the Golden Age that followed, the world came to the Arabs. Countless fortune-seeking poets, scholars, scientists, singers, artists, artisans, dancing girls, engineers, labourers and hangers-on all beat a path to the new metropolitan marvel of Baghdad, the cynosure of the world. Islam had awakened the Arab genius for civilization, by definition an intensely urban experience. The frontier-smashing warriors had paved the way for the settled sheikhs and scholars.

How did all this happen, who were these first soldiers of Islam, what did contemporaries on opposing sides of the conflict make of it and what were the lasting consequences of the conquests? These are the questions that this little book seeks to answer.

*overleaf*   Muslim pilgrims processing around the sacred Kaaba in the Great Mosque of Mecca, to which the world's 1.5 billion Muslims direct their daily prayers. The *hajj* pilgrimage is one of the five pillars of Islam.

# Mohammed
# and the Road
# to Conquest

Without Islam there would have been no Islamic conquests. And without Mohammed there would have been no Islam. Although the conquests are traditionally dated from 632 to 750, it makes sense to go back a little further. By focusing on the latter years of the Prophet Mohammed's life in particular, we can begin to discern the DNA of the conquests. Though the vast majority of the spread of Islam by Arab warriors was achieved after the death of Mohammed, it followed the distinctly martial example that he had set during his lifetime. And while the greatest phase of Islamic expansion occurred beyond the Arabian Peninsula, it was the sword-bearing Mohammed who had embarked on the first phase of conquests within it. In the process he established a number of important principles that would govern their future conduct in the later seventh and eighth centuries. These included the overriding mission to take the fight to the unbelievers (*jihad*, or holy war), how to convert to Islam, how to divide the booty and the punishment for apostasy, among other things. Within a short period of time after his death, his personal example and teachings as a leader would become absolutely critical to future Muslims across the broadest possible range of human activities, from religion and prayer to marriage and conquest. In other words, before we follow the Arab warriors on their world-changing campaigns to Syria, Palestine, Egypt, Iraq and further afield, we need to return first to the blazing sands of Arabia in the time of Mohammed.

The Mecca Mohammed was born into in 570 was, according to the later Muslim chronicles, a dark, demon-haunted place, a pagan den of iniquity and licentiousness that was home to satans, soothsayers and sorcerers. Tightly gripped between two steep mountains in a depression at the bottom of a narrow, poorly ventilated, riverless, treeless valley in a desolate corner of the Hijaz desert, forty-three miles inland from the port city of Jeddah, it was subject to stupefying summer temperatures

The Hijaz desert of Saudi Arabia, a place, according to the early Islamic poet Al Hayqatan, where 'winter and summer are equally intolerable. No waters flow… not a blade of grass on which to rest the eye'.

approaching 50 degrees Celsius – the infamous *ramdaa Makka* or burning of Mecca – and destructive flash floods brought on by violent thunderstorms, bringing epidemics in their wake. For the early Islamic poet Al Hayqatan, Mecca was a place where 'winter and summer are equally intolerable. No waters flow... not a blade of grass on which to rest the eye; no, nor hunting. Only merchants, the most despicable of professions.' Speaking to God in the Quran, Abraham described it simply as 'a valley without cultivation'. It was a settlement racked by 'suffocating heat, deadly wind, clouds of flies', according to the tenth-century Arab geographer Muqaddasi.[6] Mecca, it seems reasonable to conclude, was a pitiless, rocky, sterile, rain-starved world prone to regular famine.

Inhospitable to human settlement, Mecca, initially at least, proved hostile ground for the would-be Prophet Mohammed, a respectable forty-year-old merchant who was a member of the Quraysh, the predominant tribe in Mecca. In 610, high in a mountain cave above Mecca, he received the first of his divine

revelations. By 613, he was going one step further, preaching to Meccans, inveighing against their idolatry and polytheism, threatening the status quo in a deeply conservative society. Before the advent of Islam, each tribe worshiped its own stone effigy god, which was installed in the Haram, a sanctuary which extended in a twenty-mile radius from the Kaaba, the ancient black cube of granite. For a close-knit community bound by ancient ties of tribe and tradition, which for as long as anyone could remember had followed these pagan rites, Mohammed's teachings were dangerous anathema. His message of one God was inherently revolutionary and divisive and represented a definite challenge to the leadership of the Quraysh. They struck back firmly. Mohammed was roundly denounced as a liar, a poet, a sorcerer and a diviner. Many said he was possessed. Stung by Mohammed's insults, horrified to witness his growing band of followers – the world's first Muslims, those who had submitted to God – and infuriated by his refusal to back down, Meccans issued his uncle and protector Abu Talib a stark warning: get rid of Mohammed, or it would be war. In 619, Abu Talib and Mohammed's wife Khadija, the first person to convert to Islam, died, leaving the persecuted prophet in a perilous situation.

In the fierce summer of 622, Mohammed heard that assailants were planning to assassinate him. Desperate measures were called for. Under the cover of night he and his band of followers, including the devoted Abu Bakr, a future father-in-law of the Prophet and the first Muslim caliph, stole silently out of town and made their way to the town of Yathrib, 200 miles to the north, where local tribesmen had already assured him of a hospitable welcome. This dramatic desert journey came to be known as the *hijra*, or the migration, an event so momentous it became the starting point of the new Muslim calendar. The once Jewish town of Yathrib came to be known as Medinat al Nabi, City of the Prophet, in time abbreviated simply to Medina.

*previous pages*   Muslim pilgrims flock to the tiny, slab-roofed, graffiti-covered cave on Mount Hira, above Mecca, in which the Prophet Mohammed first received his divine revelations.

From the time of the *hijra*, military struggle, raiding missions and conquest were absolutely fundamental to the spread of Islam. Put simply, Islam would not have grown without them. It was far more likely to have remained an obscure cult in a remote desert settlement, of no interest or relevance to the wider world. At this earliest stage in the history of Islam the role of Mohammed as military leader and warrior, as much as spiritual champion and prophet, cannot be overestimated. In 624, he led a modest army – the first Muslim force in history – into the field against the Quraysh of Mecca at the Battle of Badr. Traditional Muslim accounts of the battle, none written before the ninth century, emphasize Mohammed's strategic genius and a dollop of divine intervention. Either way, Mohammed's fledgling band of Muslims prevailed over a much larger enemy in a victory that immediately elevated the Prophet from maverick renegade to revered leader of men.

Among the many extraordinary events in Arabia at this time, Mohammed's actions against the Jewish tribes of Medina stand out in the context of the conquests to follow.

To consolidate his position after the Battle of the Badr, he expelled the Jewish Qaynuqa tribe of Medina, who may have been intriguing with the merchants of Mecca behind his back. He then divided their property among his followers, retaining a fifth share for his embryonic Islamic state, immediately establishing a precedent for the division of the spoils. This was the first significant act of hostility in history between Muslims and Jews. In 625, the Jewish Nadir tribe was expelled from Medina and followed the Qaynuqa into exile after being accused of plotting to assassinate the Prophet. The tribes of Arabia had been put on notice.

In 627, the Meccans moved to snuff out the upstart Mohammed's martial and prophetic career for good, putting Medina under siege with an army estimated at 10,000. The Quraysh

*overleaf* The divinely assisted Prophet Mohammed leads his army besieging a castle in this fourteenth-century Arab miniature. From the earliest years of Islam Mohammed was as much military leader and warrior as spiritual champion and prophet.

لا اَبَدُّك لكم الآن مَطلُوكُم وَظُلِمَتُكُم لكن اَن خَرجتم مرحوم
بُون سيُوتهم بادَيِصهُم وايدى المومِنِين وكَانت مَدَّ حِصَارِه تِمصَنه
وُلادَهُم ونِسَاهُم سِتُمايةِ جَمَل مُحَمَّا الى خَيبَر لا ه كَان اوَب

وقطع جميع كلهم فقالوا فانا اخرج من بلادك فقال النبي عليه السـ
باولادكم وتكون اموالكم وسلاحكم وسلبكم فصوبا بذلك وتركوا وكا
عـ سوقا فانقعدهم عن حوالي المدينه وكان متولي الخراج محمد بن سلمه م

easily outnumbered Mohammed and his defenders, who totalled around three thousand. The two sides faced each other at the Battle of Al Khandaq (The Trench), named after the trench which Mohammed had ordered to be dug to protect the city and render the Meccan cavalry useless. The thirty-day siege collapsed amid worsening weather, Quraysh prestige – and with it Meccan trade – plummeted and Mohammed's influence and power took another giant leap forward.

After his victory at Al Khandaq, Mohammed went a step further against the Jews. Suspecting the Jewish Qurayza tribe of conspiring against him with his enemies during the siege, he moved quickly against them, besieging their neighbourhood for twenty-five days and reducing them to unconditional surrender. Mohammed's appointed arbiter, Saad ibn Muadh, then issued a terrible order. The men were to be executed, the women and children enslaved and their property divided among the Muslims. Mohammed, according to Ibn Ishaq, the eighth-century historian and earliest biographer of the Prophet, welcomed the sentence as the 'judgement of Allah'.[7] In Ibn Ishaq's account, the Prophet took charge of the mass execution personally, killing between 600 and 900.

What is especially important here is the immediate consequence of the move against the Jews in terms of liberating considerable booty. Land, property, weapons, horses and camels, together with captive women and children – some of whom could be kept, others sold on to purchase more weapons and horses – represented a massive windfall that Mohammed was able to distribute among his growing band of Muslims. He himself took a beautiful woman called Rayhana, widow of one of those who had been executed, as a concubine.

Reaping the spoils of war was not just a pleasant consequence of victory in battle. Having received divine sanction in the Quran, it was far more important than that. 'They consult you about the spoils of war. Say, "The spoils of war belong to God and the messenger." Again and again the holy book stresses this aspect of conquest. 'God has promised that you will take much booty and he has expedited that for you.' Muslims are urged to get up, go out, take up the fight and 'consume the booty that you have captured as lawful benefit'.[8] There can be no doubting the primacy of conquest, and the plunder it generated, as a driving principle in the spread of the new faith during Mohammed's lifetime – and afterwards. The overriding financial incentive was now raiding, with booty for everyone. 'In short, Muhammad had to conquer, his followers liked to conquer, and his deity told him to conquer: do we need any more?'[9]

Whatever one thinks of the decision on moral grounds, slaughtering the Qurayza Jews was politically expedient. It eliminated one of Mohammed's principal threats within Medina and demonstrated unequivocally that he would brook no opposition. Ruthlessness towards his enemies, combined with generosity towards his supporters, strengthened his reputation as a leader worth following and helped establish his credentials as *the* sacred example for Muslims for the next fourteen centuries.

It is important to note that Mohammed's martial career, almost exclusively in Arabia with the exception of some minor raids beyond it, would both inspire and provide the justification for every future generation of Islamic empire-builders, from the Rashidun 'Rightly Guided' caliphs who followed Mohammed as leaders of the Muslim world, the Umayyads of Damascus and the Abbasids of Baghdad to Timur of Samarkand, the 'Sword Arm of Islam', the Ottomans of Istanbul, Babur's Mughals and even twenty-first-century caliphate-obsessed jihadists. Among Islam's most militant adherents there are those who believe to this day that the military struggle initiated by Mohammed has not finished and should continue until the entire world has converted to the faith. In 2014, when the late Abu Bakr al

Baghdadi declared the so-called caliphate from the ancient Al Nuri Mosque in Mosul, he deliberately invoked the example of the Prophet. Later, as his short-lived 'caliphate' crumbled around him, he urged his followers on by recalling the inspirational Battle of Al Khandaq.

In 630, Mohammed marched against Mecca with an army of 10,000. It was time to bring the city to heel. Although figures from the ancient chronicles are notoriously suspect, it is clear that the army he led was huge for its time. This would have been uppermost in the mind of Abu Sufyan ibn Harb, leader of the Quraysh, who rode out to meet Mohammed outside Mecca to discuss terms. Here he was strongly encouraged to 'Submit and

A fighter from the self-styled 'Islamic State' photographed in the Syrian city of Raqqa, its headquarters, in 2014. The doomed jihadist project harked back to the idealized caliphates of the seventh century.

testify that there is no God but Allah and that Mohammed is the Prophet of God before you lose your head.'[10] Abu Sufyan, hitherto a bitter adversary, bowed his head and converted on the spot, prefiguring the conversion of his city and his tribe. The simplicity of that landmark conversion to Islam – the declaration that there is no God but Allah and Mohammed is His Prophet – has been maintained to this day, making Islam one of the easiest faiths by far to join. After Abu Sufyan's submission, resistance in the city proved minimal. Casualties were reportedly limited to twenty-eight on the Qurayshi side and just two among the Muslims, paving the way for Mohammed's extraordinary triumphal entry, one of the most important moments in the history of the Middle East. After years of hardship, controversy, struggle and bloody fighting, Mecca, the city of Mohammed's birth, became the first Muslim conquest. The Kaaba's 360 lead-strengthened idols were smashed; monotheism was the new order of the day.

The early accounts of Mohammed's actions during the conquest of Mecca depict him destroying idols, delivering justice, dividing the spoils and re-establishing the boundaries of the sanctuary around the Kaaba. They make it abundantly clear that from the outset Mohammed wielded complete political, military and religious authority. Unlike with the Christians, there was never any question within the Islamic world of rendering unto Caesar the things that belonged to Caesar and to God those that belonged to God. There was no such division between temporal and spiritual authority. In the person of first Mohammed, then the caliphs who followed him, they were united.

The Prophet's last years were devoted to uniting the quarrelling tribes of Arabia under the banner of Islam. Again this was an inherently political and military task, reinforcing Mohammed's position as the undisputed leader across the Arabian Peninsula. Islam was political, then, from its very beginnings. The armies he put into the field grew larger as the scope of his campaigns widened. At the Battle of Hunayn in 630, his army of 12,000 defeated a much larger force made up of the Hawazin tribe and their allies southeast of Mecca. The booty this time was phenomenal – armour, weapons, 24,000 camels, 6,000 prisoners – and the battle merited its own mention in the Quran.

Muslim power started to spread across the northern and eastern peninsula. Nomadic Bedouin concluded a series of agreements with Mohammed, acknowledging the suzerainty of Medina, the Muslims' political capital, and undertaking to pay the *zakat* religious tax in return for maintaining their cultural independence. In these very first days of the new faith and in the context of a traditionally raiding culture, this new levy would have felt like a protection racket, 'more a tribute to a new conqueror than a religious obligation owed to God'.[11]

Preaching to win new converts, as exemplified by Jesus, was all very well, but military conquest in the name of Allah and his Prophet Mohammed was a more compelling – and potentially highly lucrative – proposition by far. Conquest, whether peacefully accepted in spiritual submission or enforced more violently at the tip of a sword by the Prophet and his followers, was the lifeblood of Islam from the very beginning. There lay one of the most visible differences between Christian martyrs and Islamic warriors.

After a final pilgrimage to Mecca in 632, Mohammed died the same year. At the time of his death, the new faith of Islam had yet to make its mark on the world. It was still a little-known, barely understood phenomenon limited to the broiling desert towns and settlements of the Arabian Peninsula. There it might have lingered, as much a new and obligatory tribal taxation system as it was a novel, monotheistic faith.

After the death of the warrior-prophet, it was down to his immediate successors to take this new creed and spread it to the ends of the earth, thereby revealing its fundamental mission to change the world. In the life of Mohammed which they had witnessed, his followers and successors had the exemplary template for future conquest: using persuasion wherever it worked, resorting to warfare and blood-spilling when it did not. Although relatively small in scale – the Arabian Peninsula would steadily shrink into a tiny fraction, geographically speaking, of the entire Muslim world – Mohammed's earliest conquests here represented the absolutely critical foundation of far greater triumphs to come.

# Into the Holy Land:
# Syria & Palestine

Look at a map of the Arabian Peninsula. It is a wedge of land shaped like a wellington boot, or a rhinoceros head in profile. The horn is an outlying slice of Oman protruding north of Dubai, Sharjah and Ras al Khaimah, the cheek and eyes are Saudi Arabia, the throat is Yemen. To its west it is bordered by the Red Sea, which tapers slightly in its northernmost waters before forking either side of the triangular Sinai Peninsula, and which narrows again at its southernmost reach as it is squeezed into the Gulf of Aden that divides Yemen on the Arabian side from Eritrea and Djibouti on the African. The south-westernmost stretch of the Arabian Peninsula is hemmed in by the Gulf of Aden, which, as one heads further east, opens into the wide, shark-haunted Arabian Sea. Further north, forming the eastern boundary of the peninsula, is the Gulf of Oman. Follow this same stretch of water north-west, looping around the Omani headland and down the Emirati coast, and one enters what modern atlases often call the 'Persian Gulf (Arabian Gulf)', reflecting the ongoing political dispute over the name between Iran and a number of Arab countries. Geographically speaking, its name matters little. What is relevant is that these warm waters form the eastern border of Qatar, Bahrain, Saudi Arabia and Kuwait.

All of this topographical description is to make a straightforward but very important point. In the absence of a navy, if the Arab Conquests were to go anywhere from the peninsula, they were destined, by geography and the lure of nearby lucre, to go north. While a quick look at the map confirms this, the atlas can hardly do justice to the contrast between the spirit-lifting attractions of what lay north and the sheer desolation of what remained in the south. Draw a line from the Egyptian resort of Sharm al Sheikh in the west to Kuwait City in the east and the great majority of what lies beneath it on the Arabian Peninsula was – and mostly still is – a harsh, sandy, rock-strewn, waterless, treeless, occasionally mountainous landscape, bereft of permanent rivers. Dominated by the desert, sculpted beneath the fiery Arabian sun, this was a punishing environment for town dwellers, nomadic herders, Bedouin tribesmen and women, and coastal fishing communities alike. For centuries the way of life here had remained broadly the same. It was a tough existence scratched out in an inhospitable stretch of land caught in a vice between the rasping *simoom* ('poison wind') of the desert and the skin-cracking ocean, constantly harassed by the danger of ferocious raids by rival tribes, every death from which could launch a new blood feud. Men and women gave birth to new generations, from which those who survived into adulthood continued their toil, gave thanks to their God, died and were buried in shallow graves beneath the sands. This was the time-honoured rhythm of life.

And yet. Horizons during the lifetime of the Prophet had started to expand. There was no question about it. New possibilities were definitely in the air. The peninsula had found an inspirational leader, who somehow had put an end to the previously endless tribal feuding, who was leading his constantly growing band of Muslims to greater triumphs and fantastic riches under the banner of Islam – and booty for all. Change was coming. Of that there could be little doubt. Allah had already displaced Allat, Al Uzza and Manat, the three chief goddesses of Mecca, together with Hubal, a large reddish stone inside the Kaaba worshipped by the Quraysh.[12] The pagan way of life, which the tribesmen had followed since time immemorial, was over. A new order was underway.

Already Muslim armies had been flirting with the edge of the Arabian Peninsula. The ailing Mohammed, in his very last days, had ordered a military expedition against the Byzantine Empire, to avenge the Muslims' losses at the Battle of Mutah in 628, in today's Jordan, close to the border with Israel. Only his death had prevented this happening. What could be more appropriate, then, than to honour his last wishes and put an army into the field against the Unbelievers?

\*

And so, in the high, head-roasting summer of 634, just two years after Mohammed's death, an Arab army numbering five thousand reached Bab al Sharqi, the eastern gate of Damascus, put the city under siege and prepared for battle. The warriors' morale was high after a string of victories in the Levant. Earlier that summer they had triumphed decisively at the Battle of Ajnadyn in today's central Israel, the first major pitched battle between a Muslim army and the Byzantine Empire after Mohammed's death, forcing their overstretched enemies into a comprehensive withdrawal that suddenly left Palestine open to the Muslims. The prosperous city and trading entrepôt of Bostra, formerly the Roman emperor Trajan's capital of *Provincia Arabia*, later the Byzantine capital of Arabia in what is now southern Syria, had fallen, too, without much of a fight.

The Arabs standing before the ancient walls of Damascus were led by an outstanding general, who had been appointed by a no less remarkable leader. Both men had already won their spurs. Abu Bakr, father-in-law and devoted follower of the Prophet, was one of the first Muslims. He had participated in key battles, such as those at Badr, Uhud and Al Khandaq, earning a reputation for great bravery. Selected by a stormy gathering of tribesmen in Medina as the leader of the Muslims and Mohammed's successor as the first Muslim caliph, Abu Bakr had immediately faced a severe test of his authority. In the wake of Mohammed's death, a number of Arab tribes rebelled in 632 and 633, arguing that although they had submitted to the Prophet they certainly owed no allegiance to Abu Bakr. Some of these rebel tribes followed one of a trio of ambitious, self-declared

Mohammed and the Rightly Guided – Rashidun – caliphs sit at the
heart of this sixteenth-century Ottoman miniature. For Sunni
Muslims the period 632–661 was the golden age of Islam in which
God's commandments were faithfully honoured.

prophets and prophetesses operating in Arabia – Tulayha, Maslama and Sajjah. Abu Bakr launched a series of campaigns to subdue these breakaway tribes. Known as the Ridda Wars, or the Wars of Apostasy, by the spring of 633 they had resulted in the rebels' swift submission – and agreement to pay taxes to the embryonic Muslim state's headquarters at Medina. Tested to the limit, Abu Bakr had prevailed, reuniting the Arabian Peninsula under Muslim authority.

In Abu Bakr's calculation, the best, indeed only, way to maintain that hard-won unity was to raise an army of conquest, honouring the Prophet's last intentions and, perhaps more compelling, providing his warriors with fresh opportunities for self-enrichment. The choice was stark: renewed civil war within the Arabian Peninsula or holy war without. Baladhuri, the ninth-century historian, whose *Kitab Futuh al Buldun* (*Book of the Conquests of Lands*), was considered the definitive account for centuries, described Abu Bakr calling on the Arabs to rise up in a 'holy war', which would win them great 'booty'. Those who took up arms, he wrote, were actuated both by 'greed' and 'the hope of divine remuneration'.[13] These motivations echoed the Quran's promise that, 'Whoever fights in the path of God, whether he be killed or be victorious, on him shall We bestow a great reward' (4:74).

In appointing Khalid ibn Walid, an influential Qurayshi, steadfast Companion of the Prophet and the military brains behind the unification of Arabia under Mohammed, to senior military command, Abu Bakr had made a wise choice.* Time and again Khalid had shown his mettle, suppressing the Banu Hanifa and other tribes of north-eastern Arabia, before taking

---

\* The Al Sahabah, or Companions of the Prophet, were an exalted group of early Muslims, followers of Mohammed. They were those who had seen or met the Prophet or had been in his presence.

Bedouin in the Syrian hills above the ancient site of Palmyra. The conquest of Christian Syria began in the 630s and was achieved with astonishing speed. In 644, Byzantine power along the eastern Mediterranean littoral was brought to an ignominious end.

ορπεκιαυπω· εξεισωαλιροβασιλδο
μοισουμπολακεισ. πρέπεηουτουτοιω

οιοχειρουνταιαιχμαςευτοικαταςχεω· α
σαγελοιπροστηνβασιλευουσαν·

ΤΡΕΤΟΓΟΘΕΝΟΙ

the fight to the Sasanian Empire in Iraq. Khalid and his men had only arrived in Syria after making a daring and very gruelling forced march across the waterless desert. Although there is often confusion in the sources over the overall leadership of Muslim forces, exacerbated by their subdivision by tribe, each tribal formation flying its own banner and following its own leader, Khalid nevertheless stood out as an exceptional commander. Baladhuri noted that 'whenever the Muslims met for a battle, the commanders would choose him as their chief for his valour and strategy and the auspiciousness of his counsel'.[14]

Abu Bakr's appointment of other superb military commanders, such as Yazid, son of the Meccan aristocrat and Quraysh leader Abu Sufyan ibn Harb, and Amr ibn al As, 'the wily Odysseus of the early Islamic armies', was a hugely influential factor in the success of the earliest Arab Conquests.[15] Yazid campaigned with his brother Muawiya, who later inherited his military command in Syria, before becoming its governor and, from 661, leader of the Islamic Empire as the first Umayyad caliph, headquartered in Damascus. Amr ibn al As would become a legend for his heroic exploits in Egypt.

All that was yet to come. Damascus was still a Byzantine city and had been a jewel in the Hellenistic crown ever since Alexander the Great had taken it in 333 BC. Now it stood on the brink. Faced with these fierce and unknown marauders from Arabia, Damascus ultimately offered little resistance. To understand why it is necessary to go back a few decades to understand how the region's tectonic plates had shifted and the momentous consequences that followed.

In 602, eight years before Mohammed received the first of his divine revelations high in his mountain cave above Mecca, the Byzantine emperor Maurice was murdered by rebel soldiers loyal to his rival, Phocas, who declared himself emperor. Khosrow II, the opportunist Sasanian King of Kings, chose the

*previous pages*  War with the Arabs, as seen by later Byzantines in this twelfth-century edition of *Synopsis of Histories* by the Greek historian John Skylitzes.

The Byzantine emperor Heraclius (r) in battle against Khosrow II (l),
Persian King of Kings. The Byzantine–Sasanian War of 602–628
devastated both sides, creating an auspicious environment for a new
Islamic power to strike and reshape the world.

turbulent aftermath of the assassination to launch his war against the Byzantines, little knowing that it would drag on until 628. Initially the Persians carried everything before them. By 611 they had invaded Syria. Damascus fell in 612, followed by Apamea and Emesa in 613. A year later, they took Jerusalem with their Jewish allies, capturing the relics of the True Cross, the Holy Lance and the Holy Sponge and sending them back to their capital at Ctesiphon in Iraq. In the same year their forces appeared at Chalcedon opposite the ancient city walls of Constantinople, by which time the beleaguered Byzantine emperor Heraclius was minting debased silver coins bearing the desperate inscription *Deus adiuta Romanis*, 'May God help the Romans'. God took His time. By 619, the Persians had overrun Anatolia and conquered Egypt.

The Byzantine fightback began under Heraclius, who in 622 retook Anatolia, before launching a series of lighting campaigns into the Sasanian heartland, smashing the Persians at the Battle of Nineveh in northern Iraq in 627 and plundering the royal city of Dastagird and its fantastic treasures a year later. In 628, Khosrow II was overthrown in a coup by his son, Yavad II, who ordered his father's grisly murder and swiftly offered favourable peace terms to Heraclius, whose ailing empire had fought itself practically to a standstill. At a stroke the Byzantine Empire regained its lost territories and considerable prestige. Then, in a masterstroke of seventh-century strategic communications, Heraclius became the first Byzantine emperor to visit the Holy City when, on 21 March 630, he brought back the relics of the True Cross, restored from Persian capture, to Jerusalem in triumph. To cap off the brilliant Byzantine counter-offensive, the Persian Empire then descended into a ruinous civil war.

That was encouraging, of course, but not everything was so auspicious for Heraclius. Like two ageing heavyweight boxers the Byzantine and Sasanian Empires had been slugging it out on the

David battles Goliath in one of the 'David Plates', a set of nine silver platters created in Constantinople between 613 and 630. The plates reveal valuable details of seventh-century Byzantine weaponry and armour.

ropes for a generation, trading heavy blows, utterly exhausting themselves and in the process devastating and depopulating much of the Levant, already reeling from repeated bouts of the bubonic plague. To compound the crisis, a theological dispute between the imperial Chalcedonian authorities in far-off Constantinople, who professed that Christ was both divine and human, and the many Monophysites of the region, who believed Christ was solely divine, radically undermined any prospect of a united Christian response to the new Arab Muslim threat.[16] The population of Damascus, like much of the Levant, was wearied and put upon by the theological dogma – and occasionally brutal persecutions – of Byzantine rule.

With the benefit of several centuries of hindsight, the medieval Christian chroniclers sensed an impeding apocalypse. 'There was an earthquake in Palestine,' wrote Theophanes the Confessor, the tenth-century Byzantine monk and chronicler. 'And a sign called an apparition appeared in the heavens to the south, predicting the Arab conquest. It remained thirty days stretching from south to north, and it was sword-shaped.'[17]

Many apparitions are far-fetched and fanciful, yet this one proved remarkably prescient. The immediate threat to Damascus was certainly 'sword-shaped' insofar as the Islamic moniker of Khalid ibn Walid, the battle-hardened general leading the Arab conquest of Syria and Palestine, was Sayf Allah al Maslul, 'The Drawn Sword of God'. This time, though, he barely needed to draw his sword. The Byzantine official Mansur ibn Sarjun, grandfather of the theologian St John of Damascus, chose not to fight the invaders. There was, however, some confusion as to how exactly the city fell to the Muslims. Although Khalid stormed the city at Bab al Sharqi, over at Bab al Jabiya on the western side of the city the commander of the Byzantine garrison had negotiated a peaceful surrender with the commander, Abu Ubaida. After a dispute between the two generals, it was agreed that the peace

*previous pages*    The Sasanid King of Kings Ardeshir II (reigned 379–383) is crowned in this rock relief in Taq-e Bostan in Iran. The Sasanid empire, one of the world's leading powers, was a beacon of Iranian civilization before being brought crashing down by Arab armies in 651.

terms agreed by Abu Ubaida would be followed. This was a hugely important distinction. Instead of receiving a licence to slaughter and plunder, the Muslims were bound instead to honour the following guarantee to the population of Damascus.

> In the Name of Allah, the compassionate, the merciful. This is what Khalid would grant to the inhabitants of Damascus, if he enters therein: he promises to give them security for their lives, property and churches. Their city shall not be demolished; neither shall any Muslim be quartered in their houses. Thereunto we give to them the pact of Allah and the protection of his Prophet, the caliphs and the 'Believers'. So long as they pay the poll tax, nothing but good shall befall them.[18]

In this landmark document denoting the first major Byzantine city to fall to Muslim armies lay the core principles of future Arab Conquests. Security for life and property and freedom of religion in return for the payment of the *jizya* poll tax. Such a bargain, however distasteful, was nevertheless acceptable for the people of Damascus, who opened the city gates to the Arabs.

The caliph Abu Bakr, the man who had enforced unity across Arabia, did not live to see Damascus fall to his forces. He died on 23 August 634, having nominated Umar ibn al Khattab as his successor and set in motion, during his short-lived caliphate of just twenty-seven months, the Arab Conquests.

The fall of Damascus to Arab Muslim forces has rightly been called 'an event of incalculable importance', ending almost a millennium of western supremacy and returning the city to the Semitic fold.[19] In less than thirty years it was destined to become the headquarters of one of the greatest imperial adventures in history.

The two heavyweight boxers, age-old adversaries who had become totally preoccupied with their own rivalry, had failed to spot a dangerous new contender who had exploded onto the scene from the south and thrown his hat into the ring. This new force was lighter and more fleet-footed than the lumbering imperial rivals. It drew additional strength from its hard-won unity and fierce ideological commitment to the cause, a striking contrast to the political and theological divisions that had racked both Persia and Byzantium.

It is worth noting, too, when wondering how the Arabs could overcome such powerful enemies, that the Muslim warriors enjoyed no technological or numerical advantage on the battlefield. Like the enemies they faced, they routinely employed cavalry and carried swords and spears. Where they differed in one important respect was in their speed of manoeuvre. Rather like the way the pioneering mountaineers Reinhold Messner and Peter Habeler revolutionized the climbing of the world's highest peaks by their swift scaling of Everest in 1978, dispensing with the old 'siege' style of mountaineering relying on fixed ropes and oxygen in favour of a lightning, Alpine-style ascent, so the Muslims travelled fast and light, each soldier responsible for procuring and carrying his own provisions, living off the land without the slow and burdensome requirement of supply caravans. Another important way in which they appear to have contrasted with their enemies was in their willingness, indeed full-throttle enthusiasm, to die in the course of their Holy War. This energetic embrace of 'martyrdom', a tradition that harks back to the earliest days of Islam at the Battle of Badr in 624, lives on today in the rhetoric and actions of jihadists the world over.

The seventh-century Byzantine historian Theophylact Simocatta, who was writing around the time of Heraclius's counter-offensive against Khosrow II, referred to Byzantium and Persia as the 'two eyes of the world'. He could hardly have known that the Arab armies were about to give the Byzantines a permanent black eye and gouge out the Persian altogether.

*

Momentum is a strange phenomenon. Difficult to understand, it can be almost impossible to defy. Once acquired, it can appear to have a life of its own. With momentum on its side a rugby, football or cricket team, or indeed an army, can become an irresistible force, flattening anything in its way. Had the Arabs not pounced on Damascus at a uniquely propitious moment, had they invaded half a century earlier or later, rather than emerging victorious masters of a storied city that gave them a new military base outside Arabia as early as 634, it is quite possible that the Arab Conquests might never have unfolded on the grandest stage across several continents. As it was, the capture of Damascus with minimal losses was a hugely prestigious, morale-boosting victory for the Arabs that can only have sharpened the appetite for more conquest while demonstrating, in the clearest possible terms, that God was on their side. Why halt and turn back for the burning wilderness of Arabia when the going – and the prospects for more plunder – was so good?

In the summer of 636, an Arab army faced the Byzantines again at the Battle of Yarmuk, east of the Sea of Galilee. Heraclius, who had withdrawn to Antioch after the fall of Damascus, was sworn to rid Syria of these destructive invaders from the south and had assembled a mixed Greek, Armenian and Arab force. Estimating the size of the armies is predictably difficult owing to wild exaggerations by the chroniclers on both sides, but it seems possible that both armies may have numbered around twenty thousand. There was a series of skirmishes over several weeks before the final confrontation, which saw the Arabs feign a retreat to draw the Byzantines into treacherous terrain where they were then ambushed. Khalid ibn Walid organized his cavalry into smaller squadrons of around forty fighters in a novel formation intended to deceive the Byzantines over the size of Arab forces. Khalid later manoeuvred them so effectively that the Byzantine retreat, among steep ravines towards the vertiginous cliffs above the foaming Yarmuk, became a bloody catastrophe. The Arabs, wrote the eighth-century Greek Syriac chronicler and Baghdad court astrologer Theophilus of Edessa, killed so many Byzantines that their piled-up corpses formed a bridge across the river. 'Farewell oh Syria,' Heraclius was supposed to have said as he retreated from the scene of his ruin. 'And what an excellent country this is for the enemy.' It was, according to St Anastasius of Sinai, the seventh-century ascetic, monk and abbot of St Catherine's Monastery on Mount Sinai, 'the first and fearful and incurable fall of the Roman army'.[20] It also brought Christian rule in Syria to a decisive and calamitous end. Damascus has been firmly under Muslim rule ever since.

After Bostra and Damascus, the Arab momentum continued. Homs, another prosperous and significant Syrian city, fell in 637 after a hard winter's siege. Here the terms of surrender were similar to those that had been agreed in Damascus. Under the covenant agreed with the Arabs, the inhabitants of Homs were guaranteed 'security for their lives, possessions, churches and laws' in return for the not inconsiderable payment of 110,000 gold coins as tribute to the conquerors.[21] The one noticeable change in terms was a provision that the Muslims were allowed to convert a quarter of the Church of St John into a mosque, prefiguring later sharing arrangements between Christians and Muslims in the Syrian capital. These relatively painless and affordable terms go a long way to explaining the apparent ease and speed with which the Arabs 'conquered' the region. The alternative to early capitulation in the form of bloody slaughter, rapine and plunder arguably concentrated the mind, too.

With the withdrawal of the Byzantine emperor Heraclius to the north, a catalogue of towns and cities in the Syrian interior fell. They included Amman and Hama. Many, such as venerable Antioch and Apamea, chose to accept Muslim authority without a fight. Others, such as the coastal settlements of Gaza and

Caesarea, fought more determinedly. The former fell to Amr ibn al As in 637, at the outset of his enormously vigorous campaign in Egypt. The latter apparently resisted until 641 and likely fell to Muawiya ibn Sufyan, the future caliph and one of the most influential and controversial figures in the Arab Conquests. Since Caesarea had to be taken by force, rather than without resistance, the terms of its capitulation were more destructive, with many of its inhabitants enslaved and carted off back south for menial or administrative work in Arabia. On today's Lebanese coast, Beirut, Sidon and Tyre all folded without a fight. Tripoli was unique in holding out until 644, a date which marked the final demise of Byzantine power along the eastern Mediterranean littoral a mere dozen years after the death of Mohammed.

One more city remained. It was a place of historically charged holiness, sacred to Jews, Christians and Muslims alike. Jerusalem was the city of Abraham, father of the three Abrahamic faiths, of King David, Jesus and Mary. Jews revered it as the site of the First Temple, also known as Solomon's Temple, which was destroyed by the Old Testament anti-hero Nebuchadnezzar, the Jew-slaying, gold-loving despot, in 587 BC. Christians looked to Jerusalem for the two holiest sites in Christendom: the place of Jesus' crucifixion at Calvary or Golgotha and the empty tomb from which his resurrection to heaven took place. Both were contained within the Church of the Holy Sepulchre. For Muslims, Jerusalem was the holiest city outside Arabia. In the earliest days of the Muslim faith it was to Jerusalem, and not Mecca, that the believers had directed their prayers. Above all, the city had been sanctified as a bastion of the Islamic faith by the Prophet Mohammed's miraculous Night Journey, during which he had been taken by the Angel Gabriel from the sacred mosque of Mecca to 'the farthest mosque,' Al Aqsa, of Jerusalem and on into heaven, where he had met all his predecessors as prophets, received a glimpse of both heaven and hell and witnessed an enthroned God surrounded by His angels. This extraordinary nocturnal voyage was later commemorated in the inscriptions of the Dome of the Rock and Al Aqsa, both sited on the very epicentre of Jerusalem's sanctity – the Haram al Sharif, the Noble Sanctuary or Temple Mount. Jerusalem was the most sacred city within Palestine, Al Ard al Muqaddasa, the Holy Land, itself the most sacred district of the most hallowed land of Syria.

In late 636, Arab forces under Khalid ibn Walid, Abu Ubaida, Amr ibn al As and Yazid ibn Abu Sufyan put it under siege. Four months later, having seen the cities of Syria and Palestine fall one by one like dominoes to the Arabs, with supplies running dangerously low within the city walls and well aware that no assistance would be forthcoming from Heraclius after the annihilation of the Byzantine army at Yarmuk, the Patriarch Sophronius made the most difficult and devastating decision of his life. It must have come only after some desperate soul-searching and weeks of anguish, because he had made his views of the Christians' Muslim adversaries quite clear in his

sermons before and during the siege. He had railed against the 'impious and godless audacity' of the 'vengeful and God-hating Saracens' who 'boast they would conquer the entire world' and who, because of the Christians' sins, 'overrun the places which are not allowed to them, plunder cities, devastate fields, burn down villages, set on fire the holy churches, overturn the sacred monasteries and oppose the Byzantine armies arrayed against them'.[22]

There was no way out. At last, towards the end of April, Sophronius bowed to the inevitable and offered his surrender to his enemies – on condition that it be to the caliph Umar in person. The refined and highly educated ascetic, poet and patriarch found himself offering the keys to his beloved city – the 'Zion, radiant Zion of the Universe' – to an Arab dressed in filthy camel-hair clothes, mounted on a white camel and accompanied by an entourage of similarly dirty, battle-weary soldiers on camels and horses.

If Umar's sartorial style surprised and revulsed the hoary old monk, by now in his late seventies, he must have been similarly taken aback by the caliph's courtesy and restraint during their meeting. Tradition, inextricably linked with legend, has it that while Sophronius was showing him around the city, Umar asked to see the Church of the Holy Sepulchre, only for the Muslim time of prayer to coincide with his visit. Invited by the Patriarch to pray where he stood, the caliph sensitively demurred, observing that were he to do so his actions would quickly transform the church into a place of Muslim worship. He prayed nearby instead on the site of the present Mosque of Umar, built in the late twelfth century.

As is so often the case with sources dealing with the Arab Conquests, both Christian and Muslim, there are a number of different versions of the agreement reached between Sophronius and Umar. According to the prolific historian Mohammed ibn

The Church of the Holy Sepulchre in Jerusalem, a city sacred to Jews, Christians and Muslims. The church contains the two holiest sites in Christendom: the place of Jesus' crucifixion at Calvary or Golgotha and the empty tomb from which his resurrection to heaven took place.

Jarir al Tabari, the ninth-century author of the monumental *History of the Prophets and Kings* and an invaluable source on the early caliphate, the terms of this bloodless surrender were generally favourable:[23]

> In the name of God, the Merciful, the Compassionate. This is the assurance of safety which the servant of God Umar, the Commander of the Faithful, has granted to the people of Jerusalem. He has given them an assurance of safety for themselves, for their property, their churches, their crosses, the sick and the healthy of the city and for all the rituals that belong to their religion. Their churches will not be inhabited by Muslims and will not be destroyed. Neither they, nor the land on which they stand, nor their cross, nor their property will be damaged. They will not be forcibly converted. No Jew will live with them in Jerusalem. The people of Jerusalem must pay the poll tax like the people of other cities and must expel the Byzantines and the robbers... If they pay the poll tax according to their obligations, then the contents of this letter are under the covenant of God, are the responsibility of His Prophet, of the caliphs and of the faithful.[24]

The death of Heraclius in early 641, after a thirty-year reign, triggered another damaging bout of internecine struggle for the throne, thereby ensuring there would be no sustained Byzantine fightback. It also provided a final bracket to the Arabs' conquest of the Holy Land of Syria and Palestine, which had been achieved in short order through a combination of violence, persuasion, intelligence and flexibility. Underlying the campaign had been superb military organization and strategy, allied to complete conviction and commitment to the cause. The broadly generous terms of surrender offered to conquered cities, which essentially allowed normal life to resume in return for payment, were a critical factor in the speed and success of these early conquests.

It is essential to understand that, contrary to some popular views about the conquests, conversion of the unbelievers to the

*previous pages* An 1857 photo of the Court of the Mosque of Umar in Jerusalem. In the spring of 637, the caliph Umar accepted the surrender of the Holy City from its agonised Patriarch Sophronius, who had warned his flock of the 'vengeful and God-hating Saracens'.

higher truth of Islam was emphatically not the objective at this stage. The text of Umar's agreement with the people of Jerusalem – 'They will not be forcibly converted' – makes this quite clear. At the most self-interested financial level, conversion to Islam equated to a straight loss of tax revenues as far as the Muslim Arab leaders were concerned. Far better, and more lucrative, for the Muslims to allow the infidels to continue to practise their faith – and pay for the right to do so.

Over time this would change. Conquered populations from the shores of the Atlantic to the mountains of Central Asia and the Indian Subcontinent would decide to convert to Islam for a whole variety of reasons, including the financial, leaving local administrations shorn of revenues. The eighth-century Umayyad caliph Umar II (r. 717–20) would be forced to pronounce on the issue, reminding cash-strapped provincial governors of their obligations to provide equal rights to all Muslims, be they long-established Arab Muslims or brand-new converts. It is too early, however, at this point in the conquests, to talk of Arab government. That would come soon enough. First, and far more important, there was much more territory to conquer. The sacred smash-and-grab operation must continue.

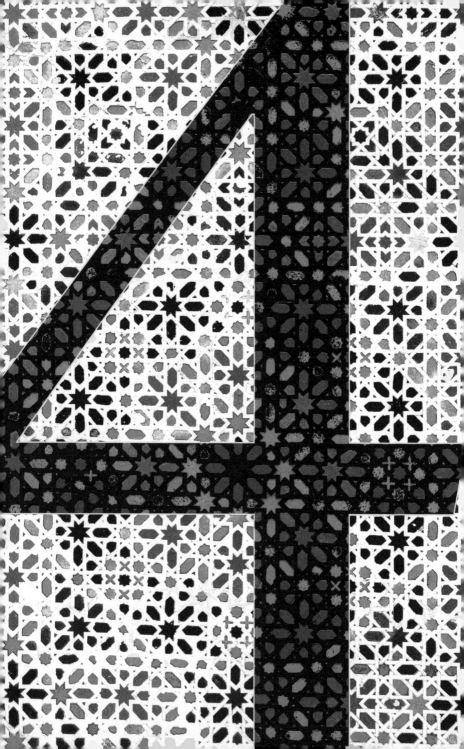

# Egypt

Like up to the great Citadel of Saladin in Cairo and you get one of the most mesmerizing views over one of the world's most frenetic, life-filled cities. Everywhere you look history explodes before you. There is ancient history, Greco-Roman history, modern history and medieval, colonial, Islamic, Coptic and Jewish. Somewhere through the smog and skyscrapers lurk the barely discernible, unfathomably ancient ruins of Memphis, twelve miles south of the almost-modern-by-comparison Great Pyramid of Cheops at Giza, built around 2467 BC. Closer to hand, running almost to the base of the Citadel, is the medieval maze of Old Cairo, in which the mighty Mosque and Madrassa of Sultan Hasan and the ninth-century Ibn Tulun Mosque, with its squat, corkscrew minaret, stand proudly pre-eminent. Southwest of the Citadel, just east of the Nile, the palm-fringed corniche and the island of Roda, there is a curiously barren expanse that turns out to be a rubble-scattered plain, scarred by unfinished excavations of villas and aqueducts, strewn with rubbish and debris from long-abandoned pottery kilns. Today these unprepossessing shards of rock are all that remain of what was, a thousand years ago, the richest city in the world.

They are, in fact, the last vestiges of Misr al Fustat, the seventh-century City of the Tents founded by the legendary Arab general Amr ibn al As after routing the Byzantines here in 641. Fustat, the precursor to Cairo, was built on the ruins of the Roman and later Byzantine garrison town of Babylon. It marks the very beginning of the landmark Arab Conquests in Egypt. Contemplating these desiccated ruins, it is difficult to imagine that Fustat was, according to the tenth-century Arab geographer Al Muqaddasi, 'the glory of Islam and the commercial centre of the universe'.[25]

At the south-westernmost limit of Fustat, north of the Ben Ezra Synagogue and a dense cluster of churches, monasteries and a basilica in the heart of Coptic Cairo, stands a single mosque, unremarkable among its fellow, much grander Cairene mosques in everything apart from the name it bears and the illustrious history that denotes. The mosque of Amr ibn al As, serially enlarged, rebuilt and restored beyond recognition over many centuries, is the first mosque in Egypt and Africa.

If we go back for a moment to the map of the Arabian Peninsula, the geographical logic of the first wave of conquests could hardly be clearer. To the north-west, Syria and Palestine, to the north, Iraq, to the north-east, Iran, and finally, to the west, Egypt, an impossibly tempting target for anyone looking for booty on an immense scale. Egypt, according to the Ancient Greek historian Herodotus, was 'the gift of the Nile', a life-producing river which irrigated prodigious harvests – every year 300 million bushels of grain were sent to Constantinople – and underpinned the reliable flow of tax remittances to imperial headquarters. Egypt had been almost entirely free from external attack for around 350 years since the late third century, a luxury which meant this indolent land of plenty was wholly unprepared for the Arab blitzkrieg.

Recent events had conspired to make this a propitious time for invasion. Just as the Levant had been devastated by the Persian onslaught in the years immediately before the first Arab Conquests, so external conflict had combined with internal strife to bring Egypt low in the early seventh century. The Persian invasion by Khosrow II's forces began in 617. Monasteries were sacked and the country, already weakened by a series of ravaging plagues, was comprehensively plundered with little resistance. By 619, the breadbasket of the Byzantine Empire had been completely brought to heel.

In an echo of the theological tensions which had torn at the fabric of the Levant, there were similar deep-seated divisions between the imperial Chalcedonian establishment in Alexandria and the majority of Coptic monks and bishops who were fiercely

*overleaf* The Mosque of Amr ibn al As in Old Cairo.
Named after the legendary Arab conqueror of Egypt, it
dates back to 641 and was the first mosque built in Africa.

anti-Chalcedonian. In the wake of a peace agreement with Persia in 629, which resulted in the withdrawal of foreign troops, these came to the fore with Constantinople's heavy-handed efforts to unite the Christian sects. When persuasion and efforts to broker a theological compromise between Diophysite Chalcedonians and Monophysite Copts collapsed in acrimony, Cyrus, the man appointed by Heraclius as orthodox Patriarch of Alexandria and governor of Egypt, resorted to more vigorous techniques, including persecution, torture and the murder of his opponents. After Benjamin, the Coptic Patriarch of Alexandria, fled, his brother Mennas was apprehended and cruelly tortured to reveal Benjamin's whereabouts. He was burned by fire and had his teeth pulled out before being drowned at sea, having steadfastly refused to give up his brother.

While Egypt devoured itself, Amr chose his moment to pounce. According to one popular Arab story, the caliph Umar, unconvinced by Amr's plan to invade Egypt, wrote him a letter after giving formal consent to the mission in which the commander was advised to turn back if he had not already entered Egypt, and only continue if he was already there. Sensing his master's ambivalence, the wily Amr deliberately delayed opening the letter until he had reached Egyptian territory in the last days of 639. Amr, like so many of the greatest Arab commanders of his day, had made a daring move. His small army of no more than four thousand, assembled from settled Yemeni tribesmen, rather than Arab Bedouin, first had to cross the Sinai before entering the challenging and unknown terrain of the delta with its defensive forces. During initial forays a number of garrison towns were besieged and taken.

Resistance was stiffer than expected at Pelusium, which guarded the eastern fringes of the delta. It fell after two months, followed by Bilbeis and Tendunias (known to the Arabs as Umm Dunayn), north-east of Babylon. The fall of the latter, reported

John of Nikiu, a seventh-century Coptic bishop whose chronicle includes considerable detail about the Arab invasion, had dire consequences across the country. 'Then a panic fell on all the cities of Egypt, and all their inhabitants took to flight, and made their way to Alexandria, abandoning all their possessions, wealth and cattle', booty that was promptly seized by the invaders.

There are controversial suggestions, from both Arab and Byzantine sources, that Egypt's Copts may have collaborated with the Arabs, scarcely surprising if true considering the entrenched sectarian divide. John hints at such collaboration with the most passing reference, his gnomic suggestion that 'people began to help the Muslims'. Some went further, he reported, turned their back on the Christian faith and – one can sense John's grimace – 'embraced the faith of the beast'.[26]

Attention quickly turned to a far greater prize. A second, larger Arab army of up to 12,000 arrived around this time under the command of Zubayr ibn al Awam, a distinguished Companion of the Prophet and battle-tested leader. These additional forces had marched along a southern route crossing northern Sinai and approaching via Suez. Their capture of Heliopolis triggered more panic and allowed a shot at the monumental Byzantine fortress town of Babylon on the east bank of the Nile, protected by walls over fifteen metres high and three metres thick, studded with stout bastions and watchtowers, some of them thirty metres in diameter. In September 640, Arab forces put it under siege and blockaded all approaches to the fortress, building a bridge over the Nile to prevent relief from Nikiu and Alexandria. Byzantine officials were arrested, confined in iron shackles and had their possessions appropriated, crops were burned, taxes on the peasantry were doubled and 'innumerable acts of violence' were perpetrated, Bishop John reported. In March 641, after months of stalemate came the news that sent shockwaves through the defenders. Heraclius, their warrior-emperor, had died, ending any lingering fancy that reinforcements might yet break the siege. Morale plummeted. In the words of Al Suyuti, the fifteenth-century Egyptian scholar, 'God broke down the power of the Romans through his death'.[27] A month later, according to one Arab version, Zubayr stormed the walls to the rallying cry of 'Allahu akbar!', forcing a rapid surrender by the Byzantine general Theodore after he had received assurances from Amr that the lives of his troops would be spared. In a final, mournful chastisement to the Christians, they evacuated the fortress on Easter Sunday, leaving considerable treasure and military equipment behind.

Tabari preserves some details of the treaty Amr struck with the Byzantine authorities at this time. Its stipulations, broadly similar to those that had been negotiated before in the Levant, granted the people of Egypt 'immunity' for their lives, religion, possessions, churches, crucifixes, land and waterways. In return, once the seasonal flooding of the Nile had finished, they were responsible for paying a *jizya* tribute amounting to 50 million dirhams, a rate that would be lowered proportionately in the event of a smaller rise in the river level.[28] Other versions mention the obligatory payment of foodstuffs by landowners, including measures of wheat, oil, honey and vinegar, indicative of the rich bounty of Egyptian agriculture that had become available to the conquerors.

The road was now clear to Alexandria. On their victorious procession to the coast, Amr's men put Bishop John's hometown of Nikiu to the sword before arriving outside the city in the early summer of 641. For the Arabian warriors, the sight of the faded yet still august city must have quickened the pulse. Alexandria, a city of glittering domes and stately palaces, the gilded Serapeum, the Cathedral of St Mark, Cleopatra's Needles (destined to be shipped off to London and New York in the nineteenth century), the citadel with Diocletian's Column and the great Pharos lighthouse of antiquity, was still one of the world's greatest cities. In the end, according to Bishop John, the end came not with a bang but a whimper. Although there was some inconclusive fighting, the fall of Alexandria came through negotiation rather than by the sword. Turmoil followed the immediate aftermath of the death of Heraclius, exacerbated by his ill-fated decision to make his eldest son Constantine co-emperor with Heraklonas, another son by his niece and wife Martina. By May, Constantine had died from tuberculosis and by September Heraklonas had been overthrown and exiled to Rhodes minus his nose, creating drift and uncertainty in which doves, who favoured a diplomatic agreement with the Arabs, contested with hawks, who wanted war. Amid this chaotic infighting, Cyrus, the Chalcedonian patriarch of Alexandria, had been sent to see what terms could be reached with the Arabs, a reversal of the late Constantine's policy of sending a relief force to Alexandria.

Bishop John shrunk the subsequent negotiations into a famously brief exchange between the two chief protagonists in Babylon around 28 November 641. Considering this moment marked the end of a millennium of Greco-Roman hegemony, the end, when it came, bordered on the bathetic. 'You have done well to come to us,' Amr told the churchman. 'God has delivered this land into your hand,' Cyrus replied. 'Let there be no enmity henceforth between you and Rome.' Although John does not provide a precise figure, the level of tribute in gold was fixed and, having taken its famous capital – possession proper began, after an eleven-month truce, on 29 September 642 – the Arabs became masters of Egypt. They were now masters, too, of a great swathe of the Mediterranean coast from Egypt to the Levant, a far cry from what had been, as recently as the late fifth century, Rome's *Mare Nostrum*.

John hints at the scale of the financial reward arising from the swift conquest of Egypt with his observation that having

*overleaf*   An aerial view of Alexandria. In 641, Cyrus, the Chalcedonian patriarch, surrendered the city of glittering domes and stately palaces to the Arab general Amr, ending a millennium of Greco-Roman hegemony.

taken the country, the Arabs 'trebled their taxes'. Under the new regime, 'the yoke they laid on the Egyptians was heavier than the yoke which had been laid on Israel by Pharaoh, whom God judged with a righteous judgement, by drowning him in the Red Sea with all his army'.[29] Perhaps this bleak verdict can partly be attributed to sour grapes, however, since evidence from surviving papyri suggest that tax collection after the Arab conquest remained broadly similar to tax collection before it. The difference was that the flow of revenues, like the vast stores of grain grown along the Nile and in the delta, was now going to Medina not Constantinople. John acknowledged that Amr took no church property and refrained from plunder.

Notwithstanding Egypt's weakness in the aftermath of the Persian invasion and the internal strife dividing the society at the time, Amr's conquest of Egypt is still breathtaking for two reasons. First, it was accomplished within a shade under two years. Second, this was no passing moment in the history of this ancient kingdom. Although it took several centuries before Arabic-speaking Muslims became a majority, with the exception of a couple of European hiccups under Napoleon at the end of the eighteenth century and the British in the later nineteenth, Egypt has been under Muslim rule ever since. Today it is, by far, the most populous Arab country with a population estimated at 100 million and counting. Amr's legacy in the built environment is hardly less impressive. Had he not chosen to found Misr al Fustat, his City of Tents, where he did, the megapolis of Cairo may never even have existed. The thrilling, visceral city we know today only came into existence as a result of Fustat's rapid, unstoppable expansion. 'I know of no city in all of Islam that is more impressive,' Muqaddasi claimed three centuries later. 'Al Fustat has eclipsed Baghdad.'

Amr's Arabs had taken an audacious gamble in marching west. The venture had paid off more swiftly and more spectacularly than the general, or his caliph Umar, could have dared dream. While the beleaguered Byzantines attributed their precipitous fall to the loss of God's favour, it was increasingly clear to the Muslims that God was firmly on their side. They had wiped the floor with the Byzantines in the Levant and now Egypt. The mighty Persians had already quailed before them. There was no reason on earth why the God-given conquests should not continue against their greatest adversary to the east.

# Iraq & Iran

On 8 August 1989, a searing summer's day in Baghdad, the Iraqi president Saddam Hussein, wearing his signature army khakis and black beret, mounted a white stallion and rode through a colossal pair of sword-bearing arms known as the Victory Arch in Grand Festivities Square, a parade ground in the heart of the city. He had invited a throng of Iraqi VIPs to the opening ceremony of this bizarre sculpture, whose purpose, according to the official invitation, was to 'announce the good news of victory to all Iraqis' on the first anniversary of their 'victory' over Iran after eight bloody years of war in which more than one million had died, half of them Iraqi, leaving the economies of two of the world's richest countries in ruins.

Designed by the Iraqi sculptors Khalid al Rahal and later Mohammed Ghani, under Saddam's close supervision, the sculpture was a Baathist Arc de Triomphe on a grand scale – the two swords crossed forty metres above the ground, where giant nets contained 2,500 helmets of defeated Iranian soldiers. To reinforce the point of Iraq's supposed victory, more Iranian helmets were embedded into the ground for Iraqis to walk on. Each 24-ton sword, made from the melted-down machine guns and tanks of Iraqi 'martyrs', was raised aloft by a 20-ton forearm, a cast of Saddam's arm enlarged forty times, commissioned from the Morris Singer foundry in Basingstoke. The swords were especially important because they were giant replicas of the legendary weapon once wielded by Saad ibn Abi Waqqas, one of the first Muslims, a Companion of the Prophet and commander of Arab forces at the history-changing Battle of Qadisiyya in 636.

Lest anyone miss the parallel between Saddam's military triumph and the Arab victory over the Persians at Qadisiyya – an unlikely prospect since, for years, the war had been known by the state-sanctioned nickname Qadisiyyat Saddam – the Iraqi dictator included two further references on the back of the invitation. One described the design of the monument: 'The ground bursts open and from it springs the arm that represents power and determination, carrying the sword of Qadisiyya. It is the arm of the Leader-President, Saddam Hussein himself...' The second was an extract from a speech Saddam made on 22 April 1985: 'We have chosen that Iraqis will pass under their fluttering flag protected by their swords which have cut through the necks of the aggressors. And so we have willed it an arch to victory, and a symbol to this Qadisiyya.'[30]

*

Around 1,353 years before Saddam rode through the Victory Arch – the exact date of the Battle of Qadisiyya remains uncertain – an Arab army of between 6,000 and 12,000, its core recruited from tribesmen from southern Arabia, faced a considerably larger Persian army commanded by Rustam Farrokhzad near a small town around 120 miles south of the future Abbasid caliphate's capital of Baghdad (the city would not be founded until 762, by the caliph Al Mansur).

Marching north from Arabia, the Arabs had made their way into the heart of Sasanian territory in Iraq to test themselves against one of the mightiest and most opulent empires in history. Unlike the desiccated desert from which they had come, this was the wondrously fertile agricultural Land between the Rivers, watered by the Euphrates through a network of canals, some of which dated back to Sumerian times from around 4,000 BC.[31] The river to the east was the Tigris, which irrigated the land to the east, along the length of modern Iraq from the Arabian desert and the gates of the Persian Gulf in the south to the snowy peaks of Kurdistan in the north. Impoverished Aramaean peasants tilled this rich land for their masters, the *dehqan* landed gentry and the nobles who administered the country for their imperial ruler, the Shahanshah King of Kings.

Qadisiyya lay on one of the main routes into the Sasanian Empire from the south-west. It was also – and this would surely have featured prominently in Muslim considerations, given their taste for acquiring booty – a significant arsenal and logistical hub.

Attractive in terms of the obvious riches it represented, Iraq was irresistible, too, thanks to the disorder and turmoil in which the Persian Empire found itself mired following Heraclius's devastating campaigns of the 620s, culminating in the worst ever rout of the Persian army at Nineveh in 627. A year later, Yavad II's coup deposing his father Khosrow II ushered in an incredibly damaging half decade of internecine strife. Yavad's swift death within six months saw his seven-year-old son Ardashir III ascend to the throne, triggering another coup in 630 by the distinguished general Shahrbaraz, the first person from outside the royal dynasty in four centuries to attempt to seize the throne. Unrest was now the order of the day. Shahrbaraz was killed in the same year, replaced by Khosrow II's daughter Boran, who was in turn temporarily deposed by one coup in 630 and another, this time fatal, in 632. That year, the boy-king Yazdgird III, who was probably eight years old, became the King of Kings, inheriting an empire in chaos. The timing could hardly have been more auspicious, then, for Arab Muslims bent on conquest.

As early as 633, a small Arab force under Khalid ibn Walid was marauding in Iraq. In a number of these initial raids prisoners were taken as slaves, enemies slaughtered and booty won. The Battle of Ullais that summer became known as the Rivers of Blood after Khalid vowed to let Sasanian blood flow in the event of his victory. To fulfil his pledge he beheaded prisoners in their droves on the banks of a canal, according to Tabari, directing the blood into watermills to bake bread for his 18,000 troops. The Arabs' first major target, however, as directed by the caliph Abu Bakr, was the ancient, prosperous and unwalled city of Hira, thirty miles south of Babylon on a branch of the Euphrates, with its population of Arab Christians and a Nestorian bishopric.* It surrendered after what sounds like desultory resistance and in the summer of 633 became the first Iraqi city to pay tribute – including 190,000 dirhams – to the conquerors. Khalid did not stay long in Iraq to capitalize on these early victories. From Medina, Abu Bakr ordered him to march east to support the campaign in Syria, which was then considered the greater prize.

Until this point, the Arab warriors had only experienced a succession of victories. They needed no other demonstration that God was on their side. Then, in the autumn of 634, disaster struck at the Battle of the Bridge. After impetuously accepting his enemy's challenge of crossing the Euphrates to do battle, the Arab commander Abu Ubayd was trampled on and killed by a Persian war elephant during the opening clashes. Again and again the Arab horses shied away in panic from the charging beasts, splitting up the Arab squadrons and driving them back onto the bridge from which many fell and were drowned in the river. After Abu Ubayd's death, Muthanna ibn Haritha, an ambitious raider from the Banu Shayban tribe of Iraq who had joined Khalid's forces to make his name and fortune, took command, but it was too late. The damage was done, the battle lost.

It is impossible to know, fifteen centuries later, what might have happened next had the vigorous Umar not become the Muslims' caliph in the summer of 634 after the death of the sexagenarian Abu Bakr. After such a punishing loss, a blow to their growing prestige and a reversal to their previously irresistible momentum, the Arabs might well have withdrawn, leaving

---

* The Nestorian Church held that the incarnate Christ has two separate natures, one human and one divine. It is named after Nestorius, patriarch of Constantinople (428–31). The Christian churches of Sasanid Persia aligned themselves with Nestorius's beliefs, which were condemned as heretical by the Councils of Ephesus (431) and Chalcedon (451).

Iraq as a Christian state of monks and monasteries, priests and churches. Umar had other ideas. During his caliphate, which lasted until his assassination in 644, there was no question of retreat or retrenchment, not even a pause for breath. Instead the conquests accelerated at an unprecedented rate so that already, within just a dozen years of the Prophet Mohammed's death, it is possible to talk about an Islamic Empire.

Umar's response to the ignominy of the Battle of the Bridge was to recruit and organize another, larger army to avenge it. He appointed Saad ibn Abi Waqqas, another Quraysh aristocrat with an impeccable Muslim pedigree, to command it. Saad was reputed to have been the first man to draw blood in the name of Islam. His mission now was to continue where Khalid had left off, extending Muslim control over Iraq, the most important Persian territory. Breadbasket of the Sasanian Empire, it was also its most productive cash cow, providing one third of the state's annual income through its taxes.

The Arab sources delight in the provocatively undiplomatic exchange between the two sides in the run-up to the showdown at Qadisiyya. In one memorable encounter, Mughira ibn Shuba, a Companion of the Prophet, tore up protocol and took his place on the throne alongside Rustam to the fury and horror of his urbane Persian courtiers. When Rustam then threatened to kill the Arabs for presuming to invade Persian territory, Mughira gave the quintessentially defiant Muslim response: 'If you kill us, we shall enter Paradise. If we kill you, you shall enter the Fire.' Asked to send a delegation in the hope of forestalling war, the Arabs declined on the grounds that this would indicate excessive respect for their Persian adversaries. They dispatched instead a single elderly Bedouin called Ribai. Setting out to treat the Arab with disdain, overawing him with the splendour of the setting, in which Rustam sat resplendent on a throne decorated with rugs and gold-fringed cushions among priceless fine carpets and cushions, the Persians watched in disbelief as this 'hairiest of Arabs' arrived on 'a hairy, short-legged mare', wearing a camel covering as his coat, fully armed with a sword inside a shabby scabbard, a spear, shield and his bow and arrows. Walking his horse over the sumptuous carpets and refusing to lay down his weapons – 'You invited me here, and if you do not want me to come as I please, I shall return' – the old man eventually dismounted, ripped apart two cushions to tether his animal, then approached the throne, deliberately pressing down on his razor-sharp spear point as he walked forward, tearing to shreds each and every carpet and cushion. Finally he sat down on the ground after plunging his spear for a final time into all the carpets around him. It was quite the entrance.

The set-piece exchanges, of course, are much later Muslim works intended to showcase the superiority and irresistible spread of Islam, the bravery of Arab warriors, the weakness and indolence of the infidel Persians, and so on. Yet they are also a brilliant window into the Arab soul and the culture of the conquests. Ribai tells Rustam that while the Persians 'attach great importance to food, clothing and drink', the Arabs 'belittle all these'. They are made of sterner stuff and are focused only on their God-given mission. Unlike the elitist Persians, a society in which nobles flaunt their wealth and power over lesser mortals, the Arabs are classless. 'The Muslims are like one body,' Ribai tells Rustam proudly. 'They are all parts of a whole. The most humble among them can promise protection on behalf of the most noble.' Mughira ibn Shuba echoes the sentiment, beginning with a direct insult to his host. 'We have heard about your moderation and self-restraint, but I think that there is no nation more excitable and stupid than you are,' he says to Rustam. 'We, the Arabs, are all equal to each other. We do not enslave each other.' A kingdom cannot be based on this Persian conduct, he warns the general.

Questioned why the Arabs had come to Iraq, the Bedouin Ribai described how God had sent the Muslims to free the world of the 'inequity' of religions and bring 'the justice of Islam' to His creatures. Peace and independence for those who submit to the new faith, certain conflict and death for those who resist. When Rustam requested time to discuss the Bedouin's offer – the by now customary formula of conversion to Islam, subjection and tribute or war – Ribai said he had three days to make up his mind. 'Choose Islam, and we shall leave you alone on your land, or choose to pay the poll tax and we shall be content and refrain from fighting you. If you do not need our help, we shall leave you alone, and if you need it, we shall protect you. Otherwise it will be war on the fourth day.'[32]

War it was. From the many confused and confusing sources it is virtually impossible to reconstruct the Battle of Qadisiyya. Even its date is uncertain, with Arab chronicles ranging from 635 to 638. Tabari reveals the importance of this single battle to the Arab Conquests by devoting more than 160 pages to the encounter, yet although his narrative teems with tales of individual valour and derring-do, quotes from the warriors and snatches of poetry, it nevertheless lacks a grand overview of the encounter. In terms of the respective sizes of the armies, too, the usual difficulties apply in making sense of the Arab sources, some of which give hugely implausible estimates. Ahmed ibn Yahya al Baladhuri, the ninth-century historian of the conquests, for example, claims Rustam's Persian army numbered 120,000 against a combined Arab force of 9,000–10,000 in what seems like a calculated attempt to magnify the Arabs' divinely assisted triumph against all the odds.

It seems clear from the accounts that the Persians used war elephants in the opening clashes, which was a serious test of Arab resolve and fighting skills. The elephants appear to have been dealt with by a combination of archers firing on the

Fought sometime between 635 and 638, the Battle of Qadisiyya was the decisive prelude to the conquest of Iraq. In this history-changing encounter, an Arab army under the command of Saad ibn Abi Waqqas routed a larger Persian force led by Rustam.

سپاه آورد بر دیده بر خود آگاه
ره مر تشته درون پر ز خون
یکی نشسته ورزین برده بران
پیش سواران سپید
چو پیش سر اندرون برد ون
بلند و بود آن زمان گرد رکاب
کمان اندر آمد ه ای سرشکاه
پر ز دل کرده گشته ای شاه
هر گز چنین روز خود جنگی همی
گوی یک تن چون دشمن جهان
دران جای خون دفن جانار
سواران کار زار سپردار نو

کسی سوی پهلوان راه
سراپای گرده ی تشیر خاک
نشان برگرفته ای نامور
سوی شاه ایران جهان نگر
سوی گردان عالمی خاص
چو بر پاده را زرمین
تیغ راه مر فوری دلخان
یکی تیغ که بر دل پهلوان
گفته ای او آن جان گاری
پراز دو دلی باز خرم سخن
درخم در زین از آن تشیر ماه
بدان سوی خون همی کار
دل گرده ز آزاد کار سروتو

تا می حسار مرد پهلوان رجیها
ترتیب کرده کنده خانه
بسی تا مور کشته شد زان داد
بسی گشت بار آورده از
ترتیب شده بندند دیگر ساری
مراد و زمین سپرد رده آخین
کفته ای نیجی بر از خون رشته
چو راز بیده پر از خون زین کنار
خرم تاج برخت شای بناز
جای سفو بر تو آزور
جای ساز از تشیر خونم جهان بین

برشته پیشش دگا
بسی تا مور کشته شد زان داد
بسی بگشت باز آورده خدم
ترتیب شده بندند دیگر سری
مراد ود بوذره زانی گشته
کفته ای نیجی بر از خون رشته
چو راز بیده پر از خون زین کنار
خرم تاج برخت شای بناز
جای سفو بر تو آزور

soldiers mounted in their howdahs, together with warriors on foot slashing the girths tied round the animals' bellies to bring the mounted Persians crashing down to the ground. There are vignettes of other foot-soldiers blinding the animals with lances and spears. It is likely, too, that the battle lasted several days, the Arabs reportedly keeping up their spirits at night by singing and dancing, reciting poetry and remembering the heroic deeds of their ancestors. Then, on the third night, which in time became known as the Night of Fury or the Night of Howling, the Arabs launched an unexpected attack under cover of darkness. By this time both sides were utterly exhausted.

Under the sudden night offensive the Persian centre gave way, Rustam was discovered and killed, his forces scattered in flight, or were cut down where they stood. Sasanian casualties were enormous, the loss of their brilliant commander, a respected statesman behind the throne, a grievous blow to the empire. 'His lion courage and bravery, his chivalry and good council, his mighty weapons and valour in war – all were gone, now that he was one with the earth,' the poet Ferdowsi mourned in the *Shahnameh*.[33]

Ultimately it was the hardiness of the Bedouin, accustomed to the indescribable hunger and fatigue of desert life, supercharged with heady doses of messianic fervour, that appears to have carried the day. Fighting in their separate tribes, each tribe commanded by its own leader, the warriors were already closely bound by ties of kin. They had grown up with each other and alongside their extended families. Sons fought shoulder to shoulder with fathers and uncles. To this powerful esprit de corps was added the no less potent fuel of faith. Commanders typically rallied their tribesmen with stirring verses from the Quran, and it was with the deafening roars of '*Allahu akbar!*' ringing in their ears that the wide-eyed warriors charged into battle. As Ibn Khaldun, the magisterial historian and master theorist on the rise and fall of empires, would write in the fourteenth century, 'The combination of a tribal solidarity and a religious drive is overwhelming.'

On a more prosaic level, Baladhuri provides another possible explanation for the Arab victory with a vignette in which a Persian veteran of the battle recalls the superiority of the Arabs' heavier arrows. 'When the Arabs sent their arrows against us, we began to shout, *"duk!" duk!"* by which we meant spindles. These spindles, however, continued to shower upon us, until we were overwhelmed. Our archer would send the arrow from his Nawakiyah bow, but it would do no more than attach itself to the garment of an Arab, whereas their arrow would tear the coat of mail and the double cuirass that we had on.'[34] Another clue to the Arab success is suggested by Tabari, who recounts the defection of substantial numbers of Persian soldiers to the Arab armies before the battle had even begun. Although it is impossible to quantify, this became a feature of the conquests in Iraq. In a curious twist of fate Saad's great victory was marred by his personal inability to fight in the battle. Suffering from ulcers on his thighs and buttocks, he commanded remotely from a castle, earning brickbats from the poets ever after. As one recalled:

> We were fighting until God granted His victory,
> while Saad took refuge at the gate of al Qadisiyya.
> We returned after many women had been widowed,
> but there is no widow among the wives of Saad!

Buttock ulcers aside, Qadisiyya became a legend of the Arab Conquests, immortalized by the Arab chroniclers even though it was a relatively small battle between two modestly sized armies. Just as the Battle of Yarmuk in 636 had spelled the end of Byzantine rule in Syria, so the crushing defeat at Qadisiyya proved fatal to a Sasanian Empire which, only a decade earlier, had been camped before the walls of Constantinople putting the Byzantine capital under siege.

The Arabs had also suffered heavy losses, but the way to Ctesiphon, the once magnificent imperial capital of the Parthian and later Sasanid Empires, was now open 100 miles to the north-east. Ctesiphon was built on the east bank of the Tigris opposite more ancient Seleucia, founded in the late fourth century BC and one of the world's greatest cities in Hellenistic and Roman times. The Arabs knew Seleucia–Ctesiphon as Al Madain, The Cities. Umar was well aware that as long as the Persians had Ctesiphon, they retained the ability to counter-attack. He gave the order for the Arab forces to continue north to end Sasanian control of Mesopotamia.

Another ancient Mesopotamian city lay en route and it was at Babylon, the capital of Nebuchadnezzar, the temple-smashing despot of the sixth century BC, that the Arabs put to the sword those Persians who had survived the rout at Qadisiyya. At Ctesiphon, the Arabs faced the immediate difficulty of crossing the Tigris in flood, without boats and with no bridges. Yet once they had been shown a route across the river downstream and had ridden their horses into the Tigris, they were able to fight off the Persian defenders who had rushed into the waters to head them off. It was the prelude to Ctesiphon's surrender without further resistance. Again, through a combination of ingenuity and tenacity, the Arabs had made themselves masters of a strategically vital city. Today the only surviving monument in Ctesiphon is the ruined Taq-e Kesra, a hugely evocative remnant of the imperial palace complex, its vast brick arch *iwan* – the largest single-span vault of unreinforced brickwork in the world – looming splendidly from the desert plain.[35]

The Persians who had evacuated the city ahead of the Arab advance carried off what they could, but they still left huge quantities of clothes, trinkets, vessels and oils 'of inestimable value', together with cattle, sheep, food and drink and other supplies laid in in preparation for a long siege. Saad ibn Abi Waqqas wasted little time turning the Great Hall of the palace, the vestiges of which still stand today, into a mosque and performed his prayers of thanks, before settling down to the equally important matter of dividing up the spoils. As ever, the Arab sources provide no end of detail about the booty and who got what, reinforcing the point that this was always a fundamental principle of conquest.

Turkish tents filled with baskets closed with leaden seals were found to contain vessels of gold and silver. There were large quantities of camphor, used as a perfume and unguent by the Persians. Baladhuri provides an amusing anecdote about the unsophisticated Arabs mistaking this hitherto unseen substance for salt and using it for cooking. Among the Persians retreating towards the safety of the Zagros Mountains, a natural barrier between the simmering Mesopotamian plains and the highlands of Iran, the Arabs spotted a detachment of soldiers going to great lengths to rescue a mule that had fallen from a bridge into the water at the Al Nahrawan canal. This determined effort to rescue a single animal aroused the Arabs' suspicion. 'And sure enough, on this mule were packed the king's finery, his clothes, gems, sword-belt and coat of mail encrusted with jewellery. The king used to wear all these when sitting in state.'[36] The royal crown was there, too, with the king's robes, brocaded with gold thread and adorned with gems. Together with the imperial regalia there was an arsenal of ornate swords, the king's fine armour (alongside the Byzantine emperor Heraclius's coat of armour and royal sword, and those of other defeated enemies), a chest containing a horse of gold with a silver bridle and saddle studded with rubies and emeralds, another containing the silver figurine of a camel with a golden, ruby-covered halter and a rider of gem-encrusted gold. For the hardy desert warriors, who had led punishingly austere lives on

*overleaf* The ruins of ancient Babylon, the capital of Nebuchadnezzar, the temple-smashing despot of the sixth century BC. It was here that the Arabs slaughtered those Persians who had survived the rout at Qadisiyya.

the Arabian Peninsula, the booty might have come from another planet. 'We have never seen anything like it,' said one incredulous Arab. 'It is not like anything we have, not even remotely.'[37]

Once Saad had sent the by now traditional fifth share, or 20 per cent, of the booty to Medina, where Umar received it, impressed both by the sheer scale of the haul and his men's honesty in sending so much back to headquarters, he distributed the remaining four-fifths to his men. Each cavalryman received 12,000 dirhams, a staggering sum of money. There was one piece of treasure which could not be divided so easily among the men. Occupying pride of place in the imperial palace was the *Bahari Kisra*, or King's Spring, a vast royal carpet of around 900 square metres, decorated with pictures of houses, roads and rivers set among orchards of fruit and vegetables and sprawling gardens teeming with flowers, all traced in gold and silver. Off it went to Medina, where Umar had less compunction about cutting it up and distributing sections among the Muslims. The Prophet's son-in-law Ali, the future caliph, was given a piece, which he promptly sold for 20,000 dirhams. 'And that was not even the best piece!' Tabari reported.

The Arabs were not yet finished in Iraq. Their advance continued northwards, pursuing the Persians all the time. Having retreated north-east after the disaster at Ctesiphon, in the spring of 637 the Persians made their last stand at Jalula, a strategically important town around ninety miles north-east of Baghdad, from which routes led to northern Iraq, Khorasan – a wide-skied region encompassing eastern Iran, parts of Afghanistan, Turkmenistan and Uzbekistan – and Azerbaijan. Fighting to retain an empire that seemed to be slipping from his hands, the emperor Yazdgird III continued his own retreat further north into the Zagros Mountains. At Jalula an Arab force under the command of Hashim ibn Utba, a Companion of the Prophet and a nephew of Saad ibn Abi Waqqas, overcame the Persian defence

The Zagros Mountains, a natural barrier between the Mesopotamian plains and the highlands of Iran. In the wake of the conquest of Iraq, Arab armies swept through this region to western Iran, where in 642 they celebrated their 'Victory of Victories' at the Battle of Nihavand.

led by the general Mihran, following repeated cavalry charges against the fortifications.

With Jalula subdued, further conquest was concentrated in the south under the command of Abu Musa al Ashaari, another Companion of the Prophet. The sources make clear that these earliest Muslims, aristocrats of the faith who predominantly hailed from the same Quraysh tribe as the Prophet Mohammed, were always favoured as commanders over those who lacked such illustrious Muslim credentials. Tabari reported, for example, how the caliph Abu Bakr never entrusted even the lowliest military command to those 'apostates' who had rebelled against him during the Ridda Wars in the immediate aftermath of Mohammed's death. The historian contemptuously dismissed those rebel leaders as 'riff-raff'. It is equally clear, too, that the quality of the Arabs' military command across the conquests writ large was a key factor in their breathtaking success. Arab commanders proved exceptional in terms of leading from the front by example, inspiring and rewarding their men and

devising highly effective and innovative strategies against their enemies.

Abu Musa next led his forces into Khuzistan, a rich and well-irrigated agricultural and textiles centre in what today is Iran's south-westernmost province, east of the Iraqi port city of Basra. It appears, from a combination of Arab sources, this time supported by an anonymous seventh-century Nestorian Christian chronicle, that once again the Arabs carried all before them, taking the fortified towns, including the famous Christian city of Gundeshapur in 638, with little resistance.

Firmly in the Arabs' sights was the venerable city of Susa, one of the oldest in the world, with a long history marked by fabulous riches, opulent palaces, bloody wars and plundering conquests. Alexander the Great was merely one of a number of famous figures to conquer the city when he sacked it in 330 BC, following in the ravaging footsteps of Hammurabi of Babylon in 1764 BC, the Neo-Assyrian king Ashurbanipal in 647 BC and Cyrus the Great in 540 BC.[38] There is a smack of the apocryphal about the Arab accounts of Susa's fall to Abu Musa's forces in 638. In one version, monks and priests were mocking the Arab besiegers from the safety of the battlements, shouting down at them: 'Hey, you Arabs, do not bother, for no one will conquer this fortress but the Antichrist, or forces that have the Antichrist in their midst.' Enraged, one of the Arab cavalrymen strode up to the gate, kicked it in his fury and shouted, 'Open up!'. Then came the miracle. 'The chains snapped, the locks broke and the other gates were opened too.'[39] Once again, the chronicles emphasize, God was on the Muslims' side.

There was more booty, much more, from the tomb of the prophet Daniel, which was seized and emptied by Arab soldiers. The saint's silver coffin was opened up and a signet ring bearing the picture of a man between two lions was discovered on the corpse. This story is mentioned by several Arab historians, including Tabari, Baladhuri, the tenth-century chronicler Ibn Hawqal and his contemporary Istakhri, the geographer. Daniel's tomb was already a local cult, which the caliph Umar had no wish to see continue. He gave orders to Abu Musa to restore the ring to the body and rebury both in the river. Irrespective of the body's disposal and the caliph's wishes, Daniel became a Muslim as well as Jewish cult figure. His tomb at Susa – several other cities, including Kirkuk, Mosul and Samarkand still lay claim to his final burial place – dominates the city today with its pine-cone-shaped tower, drawing in an endless flow of pilgrims who queue patiently to kiss the green catafalque inside.

The *Khuzistan Chronicle*, as it is known, was probably written by a high-ranking cleric no later than 660 and in its description of how the ancient fortress city of Tustar fell to the Arabs provides independent verification of the Arab sources. It relates how, after a siege of two years, a couple of men who lived in houses on the city walls made a treacherous and irresistible offer to the Arabs: "'If you give us a third of the spoil of the city, we will let you into it." They came to an agreement, dug tunnels under the walls, and let in the Arabs, who thus captured Tustar. They shed blood there as if it were water.' The exegete of the city, together with the bishop, priests, deacons and students, was killed in the holy sanctuary.[40]

The Arab Conquests by definition extended Arab and Muslim culture far beyond the Arabian Peninsula. They did this, over time, on many levels, from language and religion to architecture, literature and music. It is important to note, though, that Arab settlement in the conquered lands did not occur either immediately or haphazardly. Caliphs carefully regulated the new arrangements for warriors in newly captured foreign territory. As a rule they did not simply melt into the host community. Instead, they remained, initially at least, as a separate and undiluted Muslim community, better able to remain a united fighting force.

*overleaf* The vast brick *iwan* arch – the largest single-span vault of unreinforced brickwork in the world – of Taq-e Kesra at Ctesiphon, the once magnificent imperial capital of the Parthian and later Sasanid Empires.

In Iraq, for example, Umar gave orders for the Arabs to settle in new, specially built military encampments which later grew into fully fledged cities. The two most prominent were founded respectively by Saad ibn Abi Waqqas and Utba ibn Ghazwan, another commander and Companion of the Prophet: Kufa, which lay on the Euphrates around 110 miles south of Baghdad, and Basra, which lay close to the Shatt al Arab waterway upstream of the Persian Gulf, today closely sandwiched between Kuwait to the south and Iran to the east. Apart from its favourable location within striking distance of Medina, Kufa offered both good pasturage and a salubrious climate for the Arabs. The site of Basra offered similar advantages, at once close enough to water while lying on the periphery of the desert.

Both Kufa and Basra would become quintessentially Arab Muslim cities, architecturally focused on the twin monuments of mosque and palace at their heart, a classically Islamic expression of the inseparable union between temporal and spiritual authority. Kufa was destined to become a great centre of Islamic learning, developing expertise in Quranic teaching and the development of the *hadith*, or sayings of the Prophet Mohammed. It was the final capital of Ali ibn Abi Talib, the last of the four Rashidun caliphs, who reigned from 656 until his assassination here in 661. From that point it became the hotbed for resistance to the new Umayyad caliphate established in Damascus by the great warrior-caliph Muawiya and a powerful centre of support for the family of the Prophet, the Shiat Ali, or Followers of Ali, in time simply the Shia, who favoured a caliph descended from the Prophet's son-in-law Ali. For Shia Muslims today, it remains one of the five sacred cities in Iraq, together with Najaf, Karbala, Kadhimiya and Samarra.

Although initially much smaller, with a garrison of around one thousand men, compared with the 20,000 who settled in Kufa, the fast-growing military camp of Basra played a vital role in the conquest of Iran. By 680 its population was reckoned to be 80,000, a sure sign of the Arabs' ongoing triumphs. Less auspiciously, Basra was the site of the Battle of the Camel in 656, the first major conflict between Muslims and a landmark in the looming split within the Muslim world between what would become known as Sunni and Shia. At its heart was not so much a theological dispute as the naked struggle for power. The Sunni, the Ahl as Sunnah wal Jamaah (The People of the Traditions of the Prophet and the Consensus of the Community), preferred to choose the man best qualified to be caliph. The Shia considered Ali the first caliph and his uncrowned descendants the rightful successors of Mohammed as leaders of the Islamic world.

Such increasingly ferocious rivalry, which in time would tear at the heart of the Dar al Islam, and which still reverberates across the Muslim world today, had yet to emerge as Saad's armies consolidated their conquest of Iraq and settled down to building their new garrison towns of Kufa and Basra. Qadisiyya had dealt the Sasanian Empire a shattering blow, but there was still plenty of unfinished business in Iran.

*

When you look at the timeline of the Arab Conquests, the sheer speed with which these small mobile armies spread across the Middle East and North Africa is almost giddying. In the 630s and 640s in particular, the immediate aftermath of the Prophet's death, they rampaged from victory to victory over the once mighty Byzantines and Persians. This whirlwind of success can be hard to fathom sometimes, but look more closely at the nature of the conquests and it becomes easier to understand. Some, such as Yarmuk and Qadisiyya, were straightforward military triumphs. Elsewhere there could be more shade and nuance.

In Iran, for example, the Arabs trod much more lightly and

*overleaf* The fourth caliph Ali ibn Abi Talib kills a dragon in this fifteenth-century Persian miniature from Shiraz. Ali's reign was dominated by the First Fitna, or Islamic civil war, which ended in 661 with the overthrow of the Rashidun caliphate by Muawiya.

left a much softer footprint. In this case the chronology alone does not tell the whole story. On paper it seems scarcely credible that they should be able to conquer virtually all of Iran from 642 to 650. In practice, however, this was a different sort of conquest, less outright military bludgeoning into submission – though there was always a time and a place for that, as at Istakhr, capital of Fars – and more negotiation for tribute and cooperation with the existing Persian nobility. The ancient landowning class was well aware which way the tide was turning.

Yazdgird III had other ideas. He rallied a large army to rid Iraq of the Arabs and defend Iran from further Arab incursions, to make what effectively turned out to be the Persians' last stand. It was routed by an Arab force of around 30,000 at the Battle of Nihavand in 642. Here the Arab sources once again betray their partiality. Tabari reported that the Persian soldiers were chained together so they were unable to flee, a popular literary device intended to show that the Persians only fought because they were ordered to, whereas the courageous Arabs fought freely to spread the word of God. The booty was immense and this time included treasures from the royal family, including 'two huge baskets filled with nothing but pearls, chrysolites and rubies'.[41] The Persian defeat at Nihavand in western Iran, which Arabs celebrated as the 'Victory of Victories', brought about the final dissolution of the Sasanian state, the disintegration of the imperial army and the demise of ancient Iran. It opened the way for Arab forces to take the rest of the Iranian territories.

Resistance continued for a number of years, but it was now local and sporadic. The centre of power, where a procession of eight rulers had come to the throne in just four years, had crumbled, aided by 'the cupidity and corruption' of the politically interfering priestly class, 'the material and spiritual bankruptcy of the ruling class' and the 'stubborn and thick-headed' twenty-something monarch.[42]

A silver coin of Yazdgird III, the last Sasanid King of Kings, minted in around 634, two years after the death of the Prophet Mohammed. Most of his twenty-year reign was spent fleeing – ultimately in vain – from marauding Arab armies.

There followed his painful and ignominious flight, the titular King of Kings Yazdgird III reduced to hopping from one venerable city and province to another in the forlorn hope of raising another army to salvage a kingdom that had already gone: Hulwan–Ray–Isfahan–Istakhr–Kirman–Sistan–Khorasan. Before he breathed his last, he lived to see the debacle at Istakhr, a stronghold of Zoroastrianism, in the winter of 649. Then, the city, which had already surrendered to the Arabs earlier in the decade, rose up in rebellion, possibly on Yazdgird's instigation. In such instances, there was only one possible Arab response. Istakhr was retaken by force after fierce fighting, frantic resistance and the prolonged use of siege engines. Most of the nobility were slaughtered and the streets reportedly ran with blood. Baladhuri claimed 40,000 were slaughtered, other estimates went as implausibly high as 100,000.

The king's flight ended close to the ancient city of Merv, the easternmost bastion against the Turks of the Asian steppe, in 651. By this time the arrival of the fleeing king – complete with a retinue of four thousand non-fighters, secretaries, cooks, women, children and the elderly – was a deeply unwelcome sight for any Persian noble, including Mahoe Suri, the governor of Merv. One can easily imagine how profoundly unimpressed he must have been by Yazdgird's sudden demand for unpaid taxes. At this point, Yazdgird's general Farrokhzad, brother of Rustam Farrokhzad who had led the Persian army to defeat at Qadisiyya, mutinied and departed the scene, leaving his king to fend for himself.

The end, when it came, was appropriately feeble for a monarch who had spent most of his reign on the run – 'four years in peace and quiet and sixteen in fatigue due to the ruthless wars of the Arabs against him', as Tabari put it.[43] Mahoe instigated a plot against the king with Yazdgird's Turkish enemies. On learning of it, Yazdgird fled again, only to be stabbed to death in a watermill by the anonymous miller. Other versions of the king's demise, from having a millstone dropped on him and being choked by a bowstring, are equally inglorious. Yet, as the great poet Ferdowsi lamented, it was a tragic loss:

A man who understands the world soon says
There is no sense or wisdom in its ways:
If this is how imperial blood is spilled
And innocents like Yazdgird are killed,
The seven spheres grow weary of their roles –
No longer do they cherish mortal souls.[44]

With the spilling of Yazdgird's imperial blood, the Sasanian Empire, which had been one of the world's leading powers for almost half a millennium from 224, a beacon of Iranian civilization, expired with him. Once conquered, Iran would become a stronghold of the Muslim faith and the centre of Shia Islam. The faith's roots here deepened over the centuries as the majority Zoroastrian religion withered away, often under attack from Muslim forces subduing rebellions. Unlike other territories conquered by the Arabs, however, the cultural impact aside from faith was much less discernible. During the seventh century, Arab settlement across all of Iran was limited to Merv. This helps explain why the Arabic language, one of the most significant and enduring legacies of the Arab Conquests, never displaced the native tongues here. The overwhelming majority – 98 per cent – of Iranians today are Muslims, but Arabic is spoken by just 2 per cent of the population. The cultural influence, in fact, was reversed, and profound. High Iranian culture passed into the Islamic world as the Arabs found themselves the new masters of an ancient civilization.

*overleaf* The great Maydan-e Naqsh-e Jahan, in the Iranian city of Isfahan. Over time, Islam replaced the Zoroastrian religion. Outside religion, the cultural impact was much less discernible than in other regions. Today only two per cent of Iranians speak Arabic.

# We Need to Talk
# About Muawiya

It is a curious fact that the man at the very heart of the Arab Conquests for over four decades should remain virtually unknown in the West while being utterly reviled by many Muslims fourteen centuries later. Among those who *are* familiar with him some consider him nothing short of a political genius, a ruthless and supremely talented mastermind of Muslim conquest. On the other side are those who reckon him a godless, materialistic, usurping tyrant who plunged the Muslim world into bloody division which rages unchecked to this day. Yet however one judges his character, his actions and his qualities as a Muslim leader – and the bitter controversies which first exploded in the seventh century still rattle on today – his career remains utterly indispensable to the story of the conquests. That is why we need to talk about Muawiya.

Born in around 600, Muawiya was the son of Abu Sufyan ibn Harb, a rich Quraysh tribal leader from the Umayya clan, and his combative wife Hind bint Utba, who famously called her husband a 'fat greasy bladder of lard' for submitting to Mohammed and converting to Islam in 630. That submission, which ushered in Mecca's embrace of Islam, followed half a dozen years of the town's fierce resistance to the self-declared Prophet led by Abu Sufyan, a distant kinsman of Mohammed, and his fellow tribesmen. Precisely when Muawiya converted

to the new faith is, as so many questions remain in the distant world of early Islam, debatable. Some traditions report that he converted early, ahead of Mohammed's conquest of Mecca. Others state that he converted only at the last possible moment, out of convenience rather than conviction. Either way, in time Muawiya became sufficiently trusted by Mohammed to become one of his select group of secretaries tasked with transcribing the Prophet's divine revelations, an honoured and honourable position for the well-born youth. In time he became a junior commander in the campaigns in Syria and Palestine. Later, the caliph Abu Bakr appointed Muawiya deputy commander to his brother Yazid in Syria and, when his brother died of the plague while campaigning there, Muawiya inherited his command, the pandemic having severely thinned the ranks of other eligible commanders. Having commanded a force of several thousand at the Battle of Yarmuk, he is later mentioned in the sources as one of only four Muslim witnesses who signed the treaty of Jerusalem's surrender by Sophronius in 637 – the other three are straight from the A-list of early Muslim commanders: Khalid ibn Walid, Amr ibn al As and the astonishingly wealthy and recklessly generous Abd al Rahman ibn al Awf, devoted Companion of the Prophet and veteran of the Battle of Badr.

In 639, the caliph Umar promoted Muawiya governor of Syria, an immensely important and powerful position in the newly captured Holy Land that he occupied until 661. Had Umar not been assassinated by a Persian slave in 644, it is practically inconceivable that Muawiya would have remained governor of Syria for twenty years – the longest tenure for any governor during the period of the conquests. Umar liked to rotate his senior officials regularly to prevent them from establishing their own power base. As it was, Muawiya was able to consolidate his leading position within the emerging Islamic Empire. He was fortunate again that Umar's successor Uthman ibn Affan

A Greek inscription from the Roman baths at Hammat Gader in northern Israel. Dated to c.663, this remains the only known epigraphic evidence in the Syrian region of the caliph Muawiya, who ruled the Islamic Empire until his death in 680.

بسم الله... (نص كوفي مبكر، غير واضح تماماً)

ا ا هد و ق

و ر لا مصه

الى ـقـ ال

حد و ل ال

فا ر مو

ر كـلكـهـ ك

ا ا ل

كـكـو ا ل

سد ا ه

ا سلا ا

و سلم ل

و ا ر

الرسول الا

الله الموا

ما ملك

العلمين ولا

انا لنحن

فهل لنا شـ

ولو انا مس

هدى فهل

على سو

وا

و صـ

اهدى م

ما يشعرون

(r. 644–656) was a fellow member of the Umayya clan. Unlike his predecessors, who generally chose as commanders those with the strongest Islamic credentials, irrespective of their clans within the greater Quraysh tribe, Uthman favoured those, such as his cousin Muawiya, who had closer blood ties to him.

It was as governor of Syria that Muawiya really showed his mettle. Under Uthman his governorship expanded to include Syria, Palestine, Jordan and Hims. Later he was appointed governor of Mesopotamia, making him master of an immense swathe of land from the Negev Desert in modern Israel in the south to the mountains guarding the entrance to Anatolia and Armenia in the north. This territory produced enormous revenues which further enriched the already wealthy Muawiya. Although he was never considered a lion in battle, unlike some of his counterparts, he nevertheless demonstrated a remarkable talent for appointing brilliant commanders, which continued to serve him well as caliph while presiding over further conquests in the east from the 660s.

Around 653, he appointed Habib ibn Maslama to command his Syrian forces in a joint campaign with the army of Kufa against Armenia, earlier raids against the Byzantine territory having taken place from 640. This mission, intended to safeguard Muslim control of Mesopotamia by neutralizing the threat from Armenia to the north and creating a buffer zone between the two powers, was a resounding triumph. It resulted, first of all, in the defeat and death of the Byzantine commander Maurianos. The sources add a compelling personal detail in this story of Habib's Armenian adventures by introducing his wife on the eve of battle. When she asked her husband where she would meet him later, he replied: 'In the pavilion of Maurianos or in Paradise.'[45] By the time he had fought his way to their unlikely rendezvous, Tabari reported, Habib discovered his wife was already there. She became the first Muslim woman ever to be awarded a pavilion as

*previous pages*   A page from the so-called 'Uthman Quran', one of the oldest in the world. It is said to have been the personal copy of the eponymous caliph who was assassinated while reading it in his home in Medina in 656.

her share of the booty. More importantly, Habib's expedition led to the complete surrender by Theodore Reshtuni, the commander-in-chief, on relatively easy terms. As part of the agreement, the Muslims agreed not to garrison any troops in Armenia, while the Armenians guaranteed in return to make 15,000 cavalrymen available to the Arabs for future operations. No tribute was payable for seven years, giving the Armenians virtual autonomy, together with the assurance of Muslim military support if such were needed against the Byzantines.

Having argued for its necessity for several years, Muawiya assembled the first-ever Muslim fleet in 648 with the assistance of experienced Christian sailors and shipbuilders from the Levant, descendants of the inveterate seafaring Phoenicians. He used it immediately to invade Cyprus and impose a heavy tribute on the island a year later. The occupation of Rhodes followed in 654, giving Muawiya a strategic base from which to harry the Anatolian coast. In 655, the Muslim fleet under Muawiya's command routed the Byzantines at the Battle of the Masts off what is today the Antalyan port town of Finike in southwest Turkey. The victory over a large Christian fleet personally commanded by the emperor Constans II established, for the first time, Muslim naval supremacy in the eastern Mediterranean and was the prelude to infinitely more ambitious attempts by Muawiya on the Byzantine capital itself. The Arabs' first great naval victory, masterminded by Muawiya, was a decisive coming of age for Muslim power.

Then, in 656, disaster struck the Islamic Empire. Widely re-sented for favouring his Umayyad kinsmen, who were appointed to choice Islamic governorships, the caliph Uthman was assas-sinated in his house in Medina by Muslim rebels. Repeatedly stabbed, he bled to death while reading his beloved copy of the Quran – 'his blood spurted onto the open page,' Tabari reported. Trying to deflect a blow from an assailant's sword, his wife Naila, a Muslim convert, had her fingers cut off before the men tore away her veil, 'fondled' her and plundered the contents of the house. The Prophet's cousin and son-in-law Ali (r. 656–61), was appointed caliph in the same year, a tragic and fateful reign dominated by the First Fitna, or Islamic civil war. Muawiya, by this time a commanding authority with an army at his disposal, refused to give his allegiance to Ali. Instead he demanded revenge for the murder of his kinsman Uthman, whose blood-stained robe, together with the severed fingers of Uthman's wife – 'two with the knuckles and part of the palm, two cut off at the base and half a thumb,' Tabari helpfully notes – he hung up in the mosque in Damascus to rally his supporters.[46]

In the first major conflict between Muslims, an inconclusive but profoundly damaging series of battles was fought between those who favoured Ali and those, including the Prophet's widow Aisha, who backed the Umayyads. Ali prevailed at the Battle of the Camel in 656, named after the camel on which the Prophet's wife bravely sat in the midst of battle until it was hacked down and Aisha was captured, but when Muawiya took to the field against Ali at the Battle of Siffin in 657, the result was stalemate and many more thousands of Muslims slaughtered. By 660, when the entire Islamic project was on the brink of devouring itself, leaving both empire and faith close to collapse, the ever calculating Muawiya at last stepped forward and declared himself caliph. The stakes could hardly have been higher. His momentous task was to rebuild the disintegrating Dar al Islam.

In the end neither military confrontation nor diplomacy between the two sides carried the day. What ultimately proved decisive in this struggle for power was the poisoned-sword murder of Ali by a Kharijite assassin while he was praying in the

The first Abbasid caliph Al Saffah 'The Blood Shedder' receives oaths of loyalty on seizing power from the Umayyads in 750.

*overleaf*  The colossal walls of Constantinople raised during the reign of the Byzantine emperor Theodosius I (reigned 408–50).

mosque at Kufa in 661.* The killing of Ali, the Prophet's cherished cousin and son-in-law and the third successive caliph to be assassinated, plunged the Islamic Empire into renewed discord, inaugurating the deep division between Sunni and Shia that has riven the Muslim world ever since. On Ali's death, Muawiya, Companion of the Prophet, veteran governor of Syria, master of the largest military force in the Islamic world and self-appointed caliph, declared he would not recognize Ali's son Hasan ibn Ali as caliph. Hasan was subdued in Iraq, bought off with a generous retirement package and forced to accept Muawiya's authority within months. For the many Muslims who favoured a caliph from the *Ahl al Bayt*, the Family of the Prophet, Muawiya's ruthless move was completely reprehensible and unforgivable. Though none knew it at the time, he had founded a new, Umayyad dynasty. The era of the Rashidun, 'Rightly Guided', rulers of the Islamic world was over.

After more than twenty years as governor of Syria, effectively monarch of a state within a state, Muawiya ruled as caliph for another twenty years from 661 to 680. His sheer longevity at the highest levels of the Islamic Empire – over forty years, a third of the overall period under scrutiny – arguably places him at the very centre of this story, yet rarely has he been accorded the status he deserves as master of the conquests.

There are three main reasons for this. First, the severe discord he unleashed within the *ummah*, the Muslim community, by

---

* Kharijites, from the Arabic word for 'those who went out', were the earliest Islamic sect, separate from either Sunni or Shia Muslims. They rejected the doctrine of the caliph's infallibility and opposed the monopolization of power by one clan. They also rejected both Sunni claims to the caliphate by the Quraysh tribe and the Shia claims advanced by Ali's descendants, preferring a democratic election to the highest office. Removal of any leader who had sinned was obligatory for this puritanical movement whose fanatical beliefs fuelled regular rebellions against established authority.

The Eyüp Sultan Cemetery in Istanbul, home to the tomb of Abu Ayyub al Ansari, a Companion of the Prophet who died during one of the first Arab attempts to take Constantinople.

seizing power on the one hand and then bestowing it on his son and heir Yazid on the other. For many Muslims, especially the Shia, Muawiya was – and for many still is – a byword for tyranny, division and strife. According to this view, there was glorious unity before Muawiya, ruinous disunity ever since. Second, Muawiya dared to oppose the saintly Ali – a man described by Edward Gibbon as a rare amalgam of poet, soldier and saint – while alive and roundly abuse him when dead. In a bizarre bid to shore up the dubious legitimacy of his reign, Muawiya instituted the regular cursing of Ali during Friday congregational prayers, a practice that lasted sixty years. As he told Mughira ibn Shuba, on appointing him governor of Kufa in 661, 'Never desist from abusing and censuring Ali, from praying for God's mercy and forgiveness for Uthman, from disgracing the followers of Ali...'[47] Finally, when they came to power by the sword in 750, the Abbasids went to the most extreme lengths imaginable first to kill all male members of the Umayyad family, later to blacken their name in print.

It is important to recall for a moment the maniacal determination with which the Abbasids set out to destroy the Umayyads and their bloodline. The self-proclaimed caliph Al Saffa, the 'Shedder of Blood', revelled in living up to his name after storming Damascus. 'Hold yourselves ready, for I am the pitiless blood-shedder and the destroying avenger,' he warned. For three hours captured Umayyad commanders and soldiers were decapitated or had their throats slit on the banks of the River Futros. Buried Umayyad rulers were disinterred, exhumed corpses were 'scourged with whips and then crucified' and burned to ashes, royal skulls were used as target practice until smashed into pieces. Eighty surviving Umayyad princes were invited to a dinner of reconciliation outside the city of Jaffa and then put to the sword. Saffa reportedly sat smiling on their writhing bodies as they lay dying. 'Never have I eaten a meal that

The tomb of the controversial caliph Muawiya, founder of the Umayyad dynasty, in Bab al Saghir Cemetery, Damascus. From their imperial capital, the Umayyads ruled the Muslim world from 661 to 750.

did me such good or one that tasted more delicious,' he crowed.[48] Scholars toiling away in Abbasid Baghdad spilled torrents of ink assiduously maligning and denigrating Muawiya and the Umayyads on behalf of their imperial patrons, a tradition that survives in places today.[49]

All of which is to say that history has been hard on Muawiya. Yet if we can put to one side the question of Muawiya's controversial succession, his hostility towards Ali and the later, fully fledged sectarian division between Sunni and Shia, if we can take into account the partisan treatment of Muawiya in many of the sources and judge him solely and simply on his record of extending the Muslim world, the verdict is surely more positive.

With Muawiya as caliph the tone changed immediately. Crowned in Jerusalem, perhaps as a sympathetic, above-the-fray nod to his Christian-majority subjects that he would be an emperor for all, not just the Muslims, Muawiya had no intention of maintaining the empire's capital either at Medina, or at Kufa, which had been Ali's headquarters. Damascus suited for a number of reasons. Most important, Muawiya was on home territory here. He had developed a formidable political network, allowing him to establish the makings of a central imperial administration, the first in Islamic history. The city was also favourably located close to the Byzantine frontier in a central location between Iraq, Egypt, the Mediterranean ports and the desert of Hijaz. Returning south to the wilderness of Arabia when the Islamic world was looking north, west and east for future expansion would have been a step quite literally in the wrong direction. Instead, in another deeply controversial and contested move, Muawiya wrenched the seat of empire out of the stultifying, introverted Hijaz and thrust it into the more cosmopolitan world of the Levant. It is quite possible, as one recent historian of the city has suggested, that 'without the Damascus interlude Islam might never have become a world faith'.[50] As it was, for all the reservations about Umayyad legitimacy, the spread of Islam was without question the dynasty's longest-lasting legacy.

When it came to conquests, Muawiya proved a dynamic and restless leader who pursued his obligations of jihad against the Unbelievers with conviction, mounting at least one major military campaign against the Byzantines every year. Beyond Damascus, Muawiya's imperial strategy was to deputize leaders to take the fight to infidels in the east, beyond the River Oxus to Bukhara, Samarkand and Kabul in today's Central Asia and the Stans, while he concentrated on the Romans to the west.

In 668, only thirty-six years after the death of the Prophet, Muawiya's armies reached Chalcedon, from where they could stare across the Bosphorus at mighty Constantinople. After an unsuccessful debut siege against the triple-walled metropolis, Muawiya made another attempt in 674, launching a series of naval attacks from the Sea of Marmara that lasted several years. Still Constantinople refused to buckle. It is easy to dismiss these expeditions as abject failures, but when one considers the city only fell to the Ottoman Sultan Mehmed II in 1453, eight centuries and numerous unsuccessful attempts later, Muawiya's sheer audacity in the first century of Islam appears rather more impressive.

Active both to the north and in the east, Muawiya had further ambitions to pursue in the west. After the trailblazing conquest of Egypt by Amr ibn al As in 642, progress in North Africa had stalled. Pillaging raids into modern-day Libya had resulted in the temporary fall of Tripoli, together with the plundering of the ancient Roman settlements of Sabratha and Leptis Magna. In 647, an Arab army had defeated the Byzantines at Sbeitla in southern Tunisia, the only major engagement between the two sides in North Africa and a victory celebrated by the sources as another orgy of booty-taking in which the cavalrymen had received 3,000 gold dinars, the infantry half as much. Then, more

*overleaf*  The Great Mosque of Qairouan in Tunisia. The Muslim city was founded by Uqba ibn Nafi al Fihri in 670. He took a dim view of the local people: 'If you lay into them with the sword, they become Muslims but the moment your back is turned, they revert to their old habits and religion.'

or less nothing, bar a series of raids. It was time to do better.

In 670, Muawiya made another astute appointment by making Uqba ibn Nafi al Fihri governor of Muslim lands in North Africa. Uqba, like so many of the early Muslim commanders, was a blue-blooded Qurayshi, nephew of Amr ibn al As, veteran of his uncle's campaigns in Libya and just about a Companion of the Prophet since he had met Mohammed while a child.

The story of Uqba is one of the most romantic and swash-buckling in the entire Arab Conquests. His turbulent, high-spirited life as a roving warrior, part comeback king, part tragic martyr, was as teeming with picaresque incident – heroic victor one moment, sacked and clapped in chains the next – as Candide or Don Quixote. Unlike his boss Muawiya, his glorious reputation as a hero and martyr of the faith endures to this day, his tomb in Sidi Okba, north-eastern Algeria, receiving a steady flow of pious pilgrims seeking saintly blessings.

Uqba's first target was Ifriqiya, today's Tunisia, where in order to launch his campaign he first founded the garrison city of Qairouan, in time one of the most illustrious capitals in the Islamic world and the most enduring of the Muslims' earliest military towns. According to the thirteenth-century Arab geographer Yaqut, he did this only after first forming a very dim view of the indigenous Berber population:

> 'The people of this country are a worthless lot; if you lay into
> them with the sword, they become Muslims but the moment
> your back is turned, they revert to their old habits and religion.
> I do not think it would be a good idea for the Muslims to settle
> among them but I think it would be better to build a city here
> for the Muslims to settle in.'[51]

Uqba's permanent base at Qairouan signalled the seriousness of the Muslim project in North Africa. Raiding was not enough. Shortly after this, however, his career nosedived. Around 675 he was unceremoniously sacked from his governorship of the land he had just conquered by his replacement, Abu al Muhajir, with the partial blessing of the governor of Egypt, then thrown into chains to add to his humiliation and sent back to Damascus. Abu al Muhajir pressed on and, having converted and formed an alliance with Kasila, the most powerful Berber leader in North Africa, moved against Carthage, pinning the Byzantines back to a fast-diminishing enclave of Christian control. Imperial patronage, however, was a risky business, as governors regularly found to their cost. After Muawiya's death in 680, his son and heir Yazid reappointed Uqba to his governorship of Ifriqiya. When it came to dealing with his former nemesis Abu al Muhajir, Uqba swiftly returned the compliment, arresting him and putting him into chains alongside his Berber ally Kasila.

There was time for a last hurrah, which became the stuff of legend. Uqba headed west at speed, as the extremely patchy sources record, notching up a bewildering procession of victories as he made his way across what is today Morocco from the port city of Tangier in the north to the Atlas Mountains and deserts of the deep south. Although it was not his last moment, the enduring image of this apparently unstoppable, faith-filled warrior comes when he reached the shores of the Atlantic, riding his horse into the crashing surf until the waves lapped at its belly. Brandishing his sword, he looked towards the heavens and shouted: 'O Lord, if the sea did not stop me, I would go through the lands like Alexander the Great, defending your faith and fighting

A statue of the charismatic Arab warrior Uqba ibn Nafi al Fihri, nephew of the great commander Amr ibn al As and spearhead of the conquests in North Africa in the 670s.

the Unbelievers.'[52] In the end, it wasn't the sea that stopped Uqba, but Kasila, recently escaped from his captivity, and his army of Berbers. In around 682 the two men met in battle in what is now Algeria, where Uqba died in the great and highly profitable cause to which he had devoted his last years.

*

While Muawiya's caliphate was a benchmark for Islamic conquest, he was no less successful closer to home. By 664 he had subdued the raging Kharijite rebellion. He now threw himself into establishing a government fit for empire. While there is little administrative evidence of a centralized state emerging under the first four caliphs who ruled from Medina, under Muawiya the state-building that was required to secure an expanding Islamic Empire began in earnest.[53] Overall it was 'a very tenuous administrative skeleton for such a vast empire', simple, flexible and adaptable across the regions, but liable to 'break down during weakness, incompetence or crisis.'[54]

Muawiya recognized and recruited talent. He appointed Ziyad, a man of apparently servile birth, governor of Basra and, from around 668, Kufa, master of the caliphate's eastern dominions, including the steadily increasing territories in Iran, which were being won city by city, province by province. Ziyad proved loyal and effective while his lowly birth assured that he would never be able to win a personal following large enough to usurp his master. In the sensitive Hijaz, where Muawiya was always considered an interloper, the caliph favoured loyal Umayyad kinsmen as governors. Once appointed, governors were generally given a free hand to govern in their own style while adhering to Muawiya's broad policies as caliph. Pragmatism was the defining principle. He reorganized and reinforced the army, initiated numerous agricultural and irrigation projects, established a functioning finance ministry and instituted a regular postal service between Medina and Damascus.

Muawiya's caliphate is also highly instructive in terms of his conduct towards non-Muslims, who of course represented the overwhelming majority of his subjects. The atmosphere he deliberately fostered was one of tolerance. The Christian family of St John of Damascus, whose grandfather had negotiated the original surrender of the city to the Arabs in 634, was kept in charge of the treasury, the most important imperial office at a time when Muawiya's armies, and increasingly navy, were extending the reach of the Islamic world. When the famous cathedral of Edessa was severely damaged by an earthquake in 679, Muawiya restored it. As a Nestorian bishop in Syria put it, his Muslim overlords did not fight against the Christian religion, 'rather they protect our faith, respect our priests and saints, and offer gifts to our monasteries'.[55]

Christians continued to dominate Muawiya's court at Damascus and the chronicles are full of high-minded debates on the relative merits of Christianity and Islam. Despite his notorious reputation as a wine-drinking womanizer, Al Akhtal (the Loquacious) basked in the splendour of his position as Muawiya's court poet, jauntily sauntering through the caliph's palace with a crucifix hanging from his neck while he composed syrupy panegyrics to the Umayyads and waspish satires against their enemies. The Christian influence in that most important inner sanctum of imperial life, the caliph's bedchamber, was particularly strong. In a flagrant breach of Medinan tradition, Muawiya's favourite wife, Maysum, daughter of the chief of the powerful Jacobite Christian Kalb tribe, provided the caliph with his designated son and heir, Yazid.* A Christian also served as his

---

\* The Syriac Orthodox church, named after one of its founders, Jacob Baradaeus, a sixth-century bishop of Edessa.

*overleaf* Sistan, the largely desert region that encompasses eastern Iran and southern Afghanistan. The conquests in these remote lands, which began in the 650s and took almost a century to consolidate, were among the toughest ever fought by the Arabs.

personal physician. Tolerance and the more or less harmonious coexistence between the faiths were the bedrock of Damascus's success – as they were later of Baghdad under the Abbasids. As the monk John Penkaye, a contemporary witness from Sinjar in northern Iraq, recalled: 'Justice flourished in his time and there was great peace in the regions under his control; he allowed everyone to live as they wanted.'[56]

This favourable Christian view of the new Muslim ruler points to an absolutely fundamental aspect of the conquests. They were by no means the purely military, destructive affair that Christian apocalypses portrayed with such anguish. There were powerful elements of live-and-let-live tolerance, cultural elision and assimilation. Alongside the inducements to surrender in the form of promises to respect life, property and freedom of worship, there were also tax exemptions to those living in remote terrain. If the new *jizya* tax introduced by the Arab warriors was unwelcome, it was probably no more so than the taxes already exacted by Constantinople.

Equally important to remember is that, however foreign and bolt-from-the-blue different Islam might sound to a non-Muslim reader today, for a Middle Eastern and North African population in the seventh and eighth centuries the Islam of these horse-mounted warriors was in fact reassuringly familiar. To begin with there was the one omnipotent God of an Abrahamic faith, together with his coterie of revered prophets, then there were the prayers, scripture, fasting, almsgiving, pilgrimage to holy sites, holy days and community buildings in which to pray. 'It was different enough from Christianity and Judaism to make it distinctive, but similar enough to make it palatable.'[57] Some contemporaries, such as St John of Damascus, went even further. For John, and many of his coreligionists, Islam was less a new faith than a Christian 'heresy'. John's work, *The Fount of Knowledge*, one of the first Orthodox Christian refutations of

Islam, written at the request of the Bishop of Maiuma in Palestine, dismissed Mohammed as a 'false prophet', the Quran as a collection of 'ridiculous compositions' and Islam as 'a forerunner of the Antichrist'.[58] A clearer sign of Umayyad tolerance would be difficult to imagine.

*

With Muawiya's death in 680, the Islamic Empire lost one of its most brilliant and controversial leaders. Politically astute and militarily precocious, he was admired for his skilful leadership and *hilm*, his forbearance and self-control, and his use of subtlety and cunning to achieve his objectives. He was also famed for his eloquence, elegance and finesse, virtues that were highly prized in the Arab world. The ninth-century Arab historian Yaqubi described Muawiya's philosophy of power in a memorable passage:

> 'I apply not my lash where my tongue suffices, nor my sword where my whip is enough. And if there be one hair binding me to my fellow men I let it not break. If they pull I loosen, and if they loosen I pull.'[59]

After Muawiya had died, however, his immediate legacy began to unravel disastrously. His son and heir Yazid I was a louche, unpopular man with a love of hard-drinking, music, dancing girls and, most abominable for conservative Muslims, a pet monkey. When he became caliph, neither lashes nor swords would be able to maintain the bonds between fellow Muslims. Instead the caliphate dissolved into chaos and a second civil war that lasted a dozen years.

# From the Roof
of the World to
the Ends of the Earth

It is surely only a statement of historical fact to observe that those invaders who have been brave – or foolish – enough to attack Afghanistan in recent times have invariably been given a bloody nose. The British in the nineteenth century, followed by the Soviets in the twentieth and the Americans, British (again) and NATO in the twenty-first, have all suffered varying degrees of pain and embarrassment in their encounters with this fiercely independent and warlike mountain nation. Not for nothing has Afghanistan earned its nickname as 'the graveyard of empires'. Afghans are tough people. Their long history fending off repeated attacks from invaders near and far suggests they have had to be. Toughness notwithstanding, Ibn Battuta, the great Moroccan traveller of the fourteenth century, took a dim view of them. 'These are a powerful and violent people,' he wrote, 'and the greater part of them highway robbers.'[60]

Earlier invaders of this mountain kingdom seem to have fared rather better than their modern counterparts. Alexander the Great managed to subdue this remote corner of the Persian Empire in 330 BC, although not without being severely challenged. 'May God keep you away from the venom of the cobra, the teeth of the tiger and the revenge of the Afghans,' says a proverb attributed to him. In the early 1220s, the Mongol warlord Genghis Khan rode roughshod over Afghanistan, blazing a trail of bloody destruction while slaughtering and enslaving hordes of Afghans. In the fourteenth century it was the turn of the Turkic conqueror Timur, better known in the West as Tamerlane. He swung through from the southwest in the 1380s, announcing his arrival by razing Zarang, capital of Sistan, the then fertile Garden of Asia and the Granary of the East. Men, women and children were massacred, windmills, dykes and irrigation canals were destroyed. In time, the desert moved to reclaim what it had lost, the sands swept in and the once green province gave way to the Dasht-e Margo (Desert of Death), the Dasht-e Jahanum (Desert of Hell) and the Sar-o Tar (Place of Desolation and Emptiness). To this day the region remains poverty-stricken and deserted. Timur was back in the 1390s, traversing the snow-clad Hindu Kush mountains – known to Arab geographers as the Stony Girdles of the Earth – on a hair-raising mission to subdue the marauding Kafir tribes. At one point his soldiers had to lower the aged emperor a thousand feet over a precipice by rope. But this was holy war in the name of Islam, so everything was worth the effort. In a ringing endorsement of Islamic conquest that would surely have pleased the Prophet, Sharaf al din Ali Yazdi, the fifteenth-century Persian court historian, expressed it like this in his panegyric *Zafarnama* (*Book of Victory*):

> 'The Quran says the highest dignity man can attain is that of making war in person against the enemies of his religion. Mohammed advises the same thing, according to the tradition of the Muslim doctors: wherefore the great Timur always strove to exterminate the infidels, as much to acquire that glory, as to signalise himself by the greatness of his conquests.'[61]

Never mind that the overwhelming majority of Timur's untold millions of innocent victims were themselves Muslim. That was an inconvenient detail, but a sign, too, that conquerors then – and terrorists today – have often delved back into the era of early Islamic conquests, and selective verses from the Quran, to justify their own invasions and attacks.

By the time Genghis and Timur launched their annihilating invasions, Afghanistan was the north-easternmost redoubt of the Muslim world. And that, in turn, was thanks to the Arab Conquests which began here in the early 650s. By 653, the Arabs had subdued Zarang as part of their finishing touches to the subjugation of Iran. It became a base from which to mount more easterly raids and conquests into the unruly regions of Zabulistan, Kandahar and Kabul. However, it is a sign of the difficulties the Arabs faced here, in a remote, mountainous land that was scorched by sun in summer and blanketed by snow in winter, that the ancient city of Balkh, twelve miles north-west of today's city of Mazar-e Sharif, became the first town to fall under direct Umayyad control only in 709.

For more than half a century the pattern of the early Muslim conquests here was a relentless cycle of raiding, temporary surrender, resistance, later rebellions and, only decades later, more lasting capitulation. Even after they had surrendered apparently permanently, Afghan cities and regions were still liable to break out into open rebellion at any given moment. For example, when the Umayyads, facing an acute financial squeeze, reinstated the poll tax on new Muslim converts, the regions of Balkh, Herat and Sistan quickly revolted in the 730s and 740s. The rebellions, which spread across much of Khorasan, were a serious affront to imperial power and played an important role in the unravelling of the Umayyad project.

Taxation was one of the main causes of rebellion. In the earliest days of the conquests, the Muslim warrior elite paid no taxes. Over time, however, as the tax-burdened conquered populations saw dramatically improved prospects for themselves as Muslims, the number of converts increased significantly. In the early decades of the eighth century, tensions rose over the mass conversions to Islam by peasants across the empire, many of whom had left their land and enrolled in the army expressly to escape taxes – both the *kharaj* land tax and the *jizya* poll tax on non-Muslims. Undermined by the ensuing loss of revenues, provincial governors raised the bar for conversion, enforcing circumcision on the ranks of new Muslims and requiring them to recite the Quran to demonstrate their sincerity. In a pointed decree aimed at putting an end to these practices, which flagrantly defied Islam's egalitarian touchstone that all Muslims were equal under God, the short-lived caliph Umar II

(r. 717–20) ordered his governors to maintain equal rights for all Muslims. 'Whosoever accepts Islam, whether Christian, Jew or Zoroastrian, of those now subject to taxes and who joins himself to the body of Muslims… he shall have the same rights and duties as they have…'[62]

The First Fitna or civil war had lasted from 656 until 661, ending with the death that year of the caliph Ali and the submission of his son and heir Hasan to the arriviste Muawiya. While Muawiya could claim to have ended one civil war (his enemies would argue that he had precipitated it in the first place), his death in 680 triggered another. This time it was a much longer conflict. The Second Fitna was another struggle over the succession, which pitted the supporters of Ali's family – the Shia or Alids – against those supporting, even while holding their noses, Muawiya's son and profoundly controversial heir Yazid I. It began with the fateful Battle of Karbala in 680, in which a small army led by the late caliph Ali's son Husayn, grandson of the Prophet, was defeated by Umayyad forces loyal to the new caliph Yazid. Husayn was martyred and beheaded and it was from this point that the growing sectarian split between Sunni and Shia firmly took root. A series of battles between the Umayyads and rebels loyal to Ali's cause was only brought to an end in 692 when a Syrian army of seven thousand crushed and killed the rebel and self-proclaimed 'caliph' Abdullah ibn al Zubayr in the siege of Mecca, which caused great damage to the shrine and witnessed the low point of Umayyad siege engines hurling stones – and a dead dog – at the Kaaba (the rebels were so famished they ate it).

The man who led that operation to liquidate the rebels was Al Hajjaj ibn Yusuf al Thaqafi, who was rewarded by the caliph Abd al Malik (r. 685–705) for his no-nonsense approach to law and order with the governorship of Iraq and the eastern lands in 694. Al Hajjaj, the most famous of the Umayyad governors, was

*overleaf* In 680 a small army led by the late caliph Ali's son Husayn, grandson of the Prophet, was defeated by Umayyad forces loyal to the new caliph Yazid at the Battle of Karbala in central Iraq. Husayn's martyrdom triggered sectarian divisions between Sunni and Shia Muslims.

a loyal statesman and ruthless enforcer who brooked no dissent. 'O people of Iraq!' he thundered from the pulpit of the Kufa mosque at the outset of a campaign to bring Kharijite rebels to heel. 'I see among you heads ripe for harvest. The time of harvest has arrived and I am the harvester. Blood will soon flow below the turbans and above the beards.'[63] Al Hajjaj was true to his word. The rebels' blood duly flowed and the rebellion was quashed in 696.

With the second civil war finished and uprisings in Iraq at last suppressed, conquests could resume in greater earnest. In 698, Al Hajjaj appointed Ubayd Allah ibn Abi Bakra to lead the so-called 'Army of Destruction' against the recalcitrant Zunbil dynasty ruling over southern Afghanistan. Ubayd Allah had a less illustrious pedigree than his boss. Son of an Ethiopian slave who had converted to Islam in 630, he proved to be the Milo Minderbinder of his army (worse, in fact, since he was its commander, not a junior officer on the make).[64] Facing an enemy forever disappearing into the mountains, Ubayd Allah pressed deeper and deeper into Zunbil territory until, exhausted

of supplies and battered by the heat, he was forced to negotiate a humiliating tribute to his enemy, leave three of his sons as hostages and sign an assurance that he would never invade the territory again – an ignominious reversal of the all-conquering Arabs' usual practice. Retreating to his base at Bust, Ubayd Allah managed to get back safely. The same could not be said for many of his men, however, who died of thirst or starvation in their hordes. Instead of provisioning properly for his soldiers, Ubayd Allah stood accused of ripping them off by selling them grain and other supplies at excessive prices. Ultimately, just five thousand of the 20,000 men he had started out with made it back alive. Had he not died himself shortly after reaching Bust, he may well have met with a more unpleasant punishment.[65]

Al Hajjaj was not the sort of man to take this dishonourable defeat lying down. With the caliph Abd al Malik's permission, a new, generously funded army of forty thousand soldiers from Kufa and Basra was raised in around 700 under the command this time of Ibn al Ashaath, a blue-blooded Arabian aristocrat unlike his upstart predecessor. After steady rather than meteoric progress, Ibn al Ashaath fell out with Al Hajjaj over the latter's unreasonable demands for progress, triggering a serious mutiny by the so-called 'Peacock Army' that swelled into a full-scale rebellion against the Umayyads. Eventually it was subdued, and with it the power of the Iraqi nobility, bringing the conquests in southern Afghanistan to an unspectacular conclusion.

\*

The closing years of the seventh century had been more promising. Under the caliph Abd al Malik, the Islamic Empire began to feel much more Arab, culturally speaking. Arabic was instituted as the official language of administration, an act of enormous and lasting significance, although it is questionable

Shia Muslims chanting and self-flagellating as they march through the streets of Nabatieh, Lebanon, on the Day of Ashura, an annual Shia festival mourning the death of Imam Husayn at the Battle of Karbala.

that it happened quite in the way that Baladhuri reported: 'The reason was that a Greek clerk desiring to write something and finding no ink urinated in the inkstand. Hearing this, Abd al Malik punished the man and gave orders... to change the language of the registers.'[66] Over time Arabic replaced Aramaic as the written and spoken idiom and Greek and Pahlavi as the language of administration and financial affairs.[*]

Abd al Malik stamped his own mark in other important ways, issuing his own coinage of golden dinars and silver dirhams to replace the Byzantine denarius and Iraqi issues and building the magnificent Qubba al Sakhra, the Dome of the Rock, to mark the spot in Jerusalem where the Prophet ascended to heaven accompanied by the angel Gabriel. It was a calculated display of one-upmanship over the Christians' Church of the Holy Sepulchre, which its lofty, dazzling dome completely eclipsed.[67] In the heart of the Umayyad Empire in Damascus, after six unsatisfactory decades in which Muslims had been forced to share a place of prayer with their Christian subjects while enviously admiring the Church of St John the Baptist, Islam's pre-eminence was finally enshrined in stone by the caliph Walid (r. 705–15). In 706 he threw financial caution to the wind and built the sublime Umayyad Mosque at a reported cost of 600,000–1,000,000 dinars, several times the annual income to the treasury from the *kharaj* land tax. It became an instant architectural paragon right across the Muslim world, a benchmark for several centuries from Iraq to India, Andalusia to Afghanistan, Cordoba to Cairo and Isfahan to Ghazni. As late as the thirteenth and fourteenth centuries, the Umayyad Mosque was influencing imperial Mamluk architecture in Egypt and the Levant. Yet its exorbitant cost scandalized many and caused such

----

[*]   Pahlavi was a Middle Persian language, an Aramaic-based writing system used in Persia from around the middle of the fifth century BC.

The Umayyad caliph Abd al Malik reigned 685–705. A key figure in the development of the Islamic Empire, he expanded the conquests, issued his own silver and gold coinage, instituted Arabic as the official language and built the Dome of the Rock in Jerusalem.

disquiet that even a generation later the short-lived Umayyad caliph Yazid III (r. 744) felt obliged on his accession to pledge not to launch any grandiose and expensive construction projects.

Cracks were beginning to appear in the Umayyads' authority, whispers against what was starting to feel like a family business were growing in number, but the conquests continued. The irrepressible Al Hajjaj sent a force south led by his teenaged kinsman, Mohammed ibn al Qasim, to conquer Sind and Multan, the lower Indus Valley in present-day Pakistan. It is not difficult to see why it represented an enormously tempting target for booty-seeking Muslim warriors because this was 'the land of gold and of commerce, of medicaments and simples, of sweetmeats and resources, of rice, bananas and wondrous things'.[68] It is difficult to know exactly how the campaign began because this chapter of one of the most remote conquests is only patchily recorded, but the *casus belli* may have been Raja Dahir, the ruler of Sind, sheltering pirates who had attacked Muslim shipping. An army with a core of six thousand battle-hardened Syrian soldiers was raised in Shiraz and marched east towards Sind. Daybul, at the mouth of the Indus, fell after a punishing barrage from the Arabs' siege engines, prelude to the destruction of its temple, the execution of its priests and a terrible, citywide massacre lasting three days. Mohammed ibn al Qasim was following his instructions from Al Hajjaj to the letter:

> My ruling is given: Kill anyone belonging to the combatants; arrest their sons and daughters for hostages and imprison them. Whoever does not fight against us… grant them safety and settle their tribute as protected people.[69]

From Daybul the youthful conqueror proceeded inland along the Indus, his progress assisted by the avowedly pacifist Buddhist population, monks often negotiating the surrender of towns and cities after the Hindu warrior caste had maintained a determined

*previous pages*　Built by the caliph Walid in 706, the sublime Umayyad Mosque became the fourth holiest site for Muslims after those in Mecca, Medina and Jerusalem and an architectural paragon across the Islamic world from Iraq to India, Cordoba to Cairo.

resistance. Eventually Dahir was run down and killed in a fierce battle, causing the women of his royal household to commit mass suicide and putting an end to Sind's resistance. Multan, in today's southern Punjab, fell after another gruelling siege, its garrison routinely slaughtered, its treasuries of gold plundered. This marked the limits of Umayyad expansion into the Subcontinent.

It would be wrong to see the Arab conquest of Sind as no more than a carnival of destruction. Although initially regarded as quintessential idolaters, the Hindus and Buddhists came to be seen as *dhimmi,* protected persons, like Christians and Jews, and in return for the *jizya* poll tax were allowed to continue practising their faith unmolested. Administrative structures persisted, cultural traditions and languages survived intact and later generations of Indians came to view Mohammed as a tolerant leader, while for the Arabs he was a hero of the conquests and founder of Islam on the Indian Subcontinent. For all his achievements in the field, however, Mohammed was not immune from the wider political machinations in Damascus. The deaths of Al Hajjaj in 714 and the caliph Walid a year later removed his patrons and the new regime saw fit to order him back to Iraq where he was imprisoned and tortured, no doubt to reveal the whereabouts of the spectacular fortune he had amassed. According to one account, Al Hajjaj had invested 60 million dirhams in the Sind expedition and had received 120 million dirhams as his personal share of the booty alone. Mohammed's unhappy death behind bars brought the conquest of Sind to an end.

*

On the base of the regimental clock tower at Stirling Lines, the Herefordshire headquarters of Britain's Special Air Service, a plaque carries some verses from *The Golden Journey to*

*overleaf* The Dome of the Rock in Jerusalem, Muslim one-upmanship set in stone. The Arab geographer Muqaddasi suggested that Abd al Malik, seeing the Dome of the Holy Sepulchre, 'was concerned lest it dazzle the thoughts of the Muslims, and thus he erected above the Rock the Dome'.

*Samarkand* by James Elroy Flecker, the English novelist and playwright.

> We are the Pilgrims, master; we shall go
> Always a little further: it may be
> Beyond that last blue mountain barred with snow
> Across that angry or that glimmering sea...

While these lines capture the ethos of Britain's elite special forces, they unmistakably echo the insatiable spirit of the Arab Conquests, that desire to 'go always a little further'. And, however inadvertently, these words from 'the pilgrims' also pick up on the Arabs' mission in Central Asia, as they boast, 'surely we are brave, / Who take the golden road to Samarkand.'

The Arabs had occupied Khorasan since 650 and during the following half century had extended their control of the lands up to the banks of the Oxus, or Amu Darya. Directly across those foaming waters lay what the Arabs called Mawarannahr, literally 'What is Beyond the River' – a vast swathe of land including some noble and rich cities of antiquity: Samarkand, Bukhara, Termez, Balkh, Urganch and Khiva. The Persian king Cyrus the Great had captured Samarkand in around 550 BC, a conquest followed by Alexander, who took Marakanda, as the Greeks knew it, in 329 BC.

On a modern atlas Mawarannahr extends across the cotton basket of the former Soviet Union, the independent Central Asian republics of Uzbekistan, Kazakhstan, Turkmenistan, Tajikistan and Kyrgyzstan, running into north-west Xinjiang in China. The territory was also known as Transoxiana, whose centre was a three-hundred-mile-wide corridor of land sandwiched between the two greatest rivers of Central Asia, the Amu Darya and Syr Darya. Better known by their more evocative classical names, the Oxus and the Jaxartes, these were two of the four medieval rivers of paradise, slivers of fertility rushing through an otherwise

The ancient city of Balkh in northern Afghanistan, known to Arabs as the 'Mother of Cities', was the first city in the region to fall under direct Umayyad control as late as 709.

barren landscape. At 1,800 miles, the Amu Darya is the region's longest, sweeping west in a gentle arc from the Pamir mountains before checking north-west towards the southern tip of the Aral Sea. The Syr Darya, 1,400 miles long, flows west from the snow-covered Tien Shan mountains before it, too, diverts north-west, though it no longer waters the devastatingly shrunken Aral Sea on its northern shores. Beyond the rivers were the deadly sands and rasping winds of the desert. West of the Amu Darya stretched the spirit-shattering wilderness of the Qara Qum (Black Sands) desert. East of the Syr Darya, the equally inhospitable Hunger Steppe unfurled, an unfathomable plateau melting into the horizon.

Another campaign in another territory called for another Muslim commander. Al Hajjaj appointed Qutayba ibn Muslim, a leader who had impressed him during the suppression of Ibn al Ashaath's revolt, after which he had been appointed governor of the city of Ray in northern Iran. In 705 Qutayba was promoted to governor of Khorasan. In his first speech to his soldiers,

according to an eyewitness quoted by Tabari, he voiced the conquerors' sacred smash-and-grab creed:

> 'God has caused you to alight in this place so that He may make his religion strong, protect sacred things by means of you, and through you increase the abundance of wealth and the meting out of harsh treatment to the enemy.'[70]

His warning that the men should get used to 'the greatest of distances and the sharpest of pains' was astute. Unlike some of the other conquests, such as those in Egypt and the Maghreb, this would be some of the most testing campaigning the Arabs had ever experienced. After surrendering, only then to rebel and kill Qutayba's governor on the Arabs' departure, Paykand, City of Merchants, in the province of Sogdia, was the first to feel Qutayba's wrath. Determined to send a message, he killed all surviving soldiers, enslaved the women and children and, with

Al Hajjaj's permission, distributed enormous quantities of booty among his men, including melted down gold and silver bullion weighing up to 150,000 *mithqals*, around 660 kg.[71] In 707 and 708, Qutayba was unable to press home this early advantage following concerted resistance from the Sogdians, now allied with the Turkish tribes of the steppe. Unimpressed by his subordinate, to whom he sent a stiff reprimand with instructions to repent to God and buck up his ideas, Hajjaj ordered Qutayba to launch a lightning attack on Bukhara. It was a close-fought affair. At one point, the chronicles report, the Sogdians with their Turkish allies stormed into Qutayba's camp and were only fought off by the women there amid desperate scenes. A combined infantry and cavalry assault dislodged the Turks from the higher ground, the troops rallied by the promise of one hundred dirhams for each enemy head they brought back. The fall of Bukhara in 709 persuaded Tarkhun, the ruler of Samarkand, to offer his vassalage to Qutayba to avoid his city being stormed in turn, even though it took several campaigning seasons for the Arabs to subdue Bukhara completely, settle it with a permanent garrison and, in 713, build a mosque symbolically located on the site of a previous fire temple. From this point the religion of the conquerors began to acquire new followers.

Conquest here, in this land of feuding princes and principalities, was never easy or straightforward. Nizak, prince of Badghis (north-west Afghanistan), chose the aftermath of the fall of Bukhara to desert his new ally Qutayba and, with the help of fellow local rulers, mount a rebellion. As he confessed to his advisers, 'I am with this man and I don't feel safe with him, for the Arab is like a dog: if you beat him he barks and if you feed him he wags his tail. If you campaign against him and then give him something, he is pleased and forgets what you have done to him.'[72]

Qutayba did not forget. Nor did he prove as waggy-tailed as

Another ancient Central Asian city, Samarkand, 'Pearl of the East', 'Garden of the Soul', fell to the Arabs in 712. Founded in the eighth century BC, Samarkand later became the imperial, blue-domed capital of Timur, or Tamerlane, the Sword Arm of Islam.

the complacent Nizak had anticipated. Although the campaigning season was over, he dispatched a force of 12,000 under the command of his brother and right-hand man Abd al Rahman ibn Muslim to winter in Balkh. Before the spring of 710 had arrived, this army marched against the would-be rebels, crucifying a number of those they captured in a ruthless use of terror to snuff out the uprising before it had even begun. Nizak fled and holed up in the mountains north of Kabul, only surrendering to Qutayba after a siege of two months and a guarantee of safe conduct. The Arab's bite was worse than his bark. In a brutal violation of the age-old customs of pardons and safe conducts, he had Nizak executed. The rebellion was suppressed.

In 712, the elderly Tarkhun, who earlier had agreed to pay tribute to the Muslims, was ousted and a new ruler emerged in Samarkand. Ghurak was a more independent-minded man than his predecessor and determined to resist Qutayba. A night-time attack on the Arabs failed, however, in a clash in which many Sogdian nobles were killed. There followed a month-long siege during which Arab mangonels rained a barrage of missiles against the city walls, eventually forcing a breach. After more frenetic fighting, the city fell and punitive terms were agreed. Qutayba demanded 30,000 healthy slaves of fighting age – no old men or young boys among them – and a stupendous annual tribute of 2.2 million dirhams. In a calculated show of contempt for the Zoroastrian faith, he then destroyed all the fire temples, had the idols and sculptures piled up and, ignoring the entreaties of the horrified Sogdians, personally set fire to the lot of them. The melted gold and silver nails they contained weighed 50,000 mithqals, around 220 kg of bullion. Resolved to ensure Samarkand remained firmly in Muslim hands, Qutayba left a garrison of four thousand under his loyal brother's command, with orders that from now on only Muslims were permitted to stay within the ancient walls on pain of death.

The Uzbek city of Bukhara, 'Dome of Islam', fell to the Arabs in 709.
Built in 1127, in the eighteenth and nineteenth centuries the 50-metre
high Kalon Minaret became the macabre 'Tower of Death', from whose
summit criminals were thrown to their deaths.

In another sign of the Arabs' bold, world-conquering ambitions, of how they were always ready to venture 'a little further' in the cause of Islam and plunder, there are tantalising glimpses in the sources of diplomatic exchanges with the Tang court of China. Arab legend has it that Al Hajjaj offered the governorship of China to the first Arab warrior to get there. In 713 an Arab delegation caused a sensation when the envoy was presented to the emperor and flatly refused to bow before him. 'In my country we only bow to God, never to a prince,' he said. It was only the intercession of a minister, who reminded the officials that differences in court etiquette in foreign countries should not be considered a crime, that prevented the ambassador from being executed on the spot.[73]

Mohammed ibn al Qasim, hero of the conquest of Sind, had been brought low by political intrigue in Damascus. Qutayba was determined to avoid the same fate. In 715 he announced to his soldiers that he would not serve the new caliph Sulayman (r. 715–17), whose succession he had opposed. But his men – both the

Khorasan Arabs and the locally raised forces – had no appetite for rebellion. After he roundly harangued them in intemperate language for their lack of enthusiasm, they then turned against him under the leadership of a Bedouin called Waki al Tamimi. Qutayba's brother Abd al Rahman was stoned to death, Qutayba was stabbed and beheaded. It was a shabby end for another hero of the Arab Conquests and it proved the end of further progress in Transoxiana for another generation. Arab prestige and power crumbled, local revolts and Turkish invasions became the order of the day. It was only at the Battle of Talas in 751 that an Abbasid Arab army, supported by Tibetan allies and defecting Turks, routed Tang Chinese forces and decisively reasserted Muslim control over Transoxiana.

\*

While Qutayba was embarking on his gruelling campaigns in the deserts of southern Afghanistan in 711, four thousand miles to the west a fellow Muslim in arms was making a very different journey in the same cause. That summer Tariq ibn Ziyad, a Berber commander, led an army across the nine-mile Straits of Gibraltar on behalf of his boss, Musa ibn Nusayr, the newly appointed Arab governor of Ifriqiya. The earliest Arab Conquests in Spain are poorly documented and the details often murky, but it appears that the Muslims had responded, less altruistically than out of self-interest, to an appeal for help in a fight for the succession between the sons of the late Visigothic king Witiza, who had died in 710, on the one hand and supporters of the rival elected king, Roderic, on the other. The first encounter between Muslims and Christians on the Iberian Peninsula came in the summer of 711 at the Battle of Guadelete, in which Roderic, along with many Visigothic nobles, was killed.

Pressing on after this rousing victory, Tariq sent some of his

*previous pages*   In 711, the Berber commander Tariq ibn Ziyad conquered Cordoba. It soon became the capital of Muslim Al Andalus, one of the most glittering jewels of Islamic civilization.

men on into the Guadalquivir valley. There they stormed the ancient city of Cordoba whose history ranges back more than two millennia to Carthaginian times.[74] Conquered by the Romans in the early third century BC, it was the capital of Hispania Baetica, the empire's southernmost province in Spain, a port city from which wheat, wine and olive oil were shipped back to Rome. In 571 the campaigning Visigothic king Leovigild took it from the Byzantines and established a bishopric here, increasing the town's prestige and importance. Long a rich agricultural centre auspiciously located between the cattle-raising territory of the Sierra Morena mountain range to the north and the fertile farming land to the south, within just a few years of its capture in 711, Cordoba – Al Qurtuba to the Muslim conquerors – had emerged as the provincial capital of Muslim Al Andalus. Those soldiers who had survived the attack were executed. Cordoba's governor was spared and sent as a trophy to the caliph Walid in Damascus. While one part of his army seized Cordoba, Tariq led a force north to conquer the royal Visigothic capital of Toledo, which was abandoned by its bishop and taken without any serious resistance.

The Visigothic kingdom was imploding. Internal tensions between the monarchy and the recalcitrant landowning nobility, who consistently refused to provide men and materiel to the royal army, had been stretched to breaking point. Taking advantage of the ruinous division into which Spain had fallen, in the summer of 712 Musa decided on all-out conquest – he couldn't let Tariq take all the glory and booty – and entered Spain with a largely Arab army of eighteen thousand men. Seville was the first great city to fold, again after only cursory resistance, quickly followed by Saragossa. Reunited with Tariq in Toledo, Musa discovered his subordinate had been doing extremely well – too well, in fact – for himself. In particular he demanded the so-called Table of Solomon, lavishly made from bejewelled gold and silver. Tariq

*overleaf*  The forest of 856 columns – marble, jasper, onyx and graphite – inside the eighth-century Great Mosque of Cordoba, known to most Spaniards as Santa Iglesia Catedral or, less triumphantly, as the Mezquita-Catedral.

grudgingly handed it over to his boss, though not before having removed a leg and substituted a less valuable one in its place.

The mid-eighth-century *Chronicle of 754*, written by an anonymous Christian under Muslim rule, captures the tone of bitter defeat, accusing Musa of imposing 'an evil and fraudulent peace' on the peninsula, publicly decapitating nobles and exposing Hispania to 'the sword, famine and captivity. Musa ruined beautiful cities, burning them with fire; condemned lords and powerful men to the cross and butchered youths and infants with the sword.'[75]

The Jews and Christians of Spain had no reason to believe that this was anything other than a lightning raid, the baleful results of which would eventually pass. They can scarcely have imagined that Muslims would rule most of the peninsula for the next eight centuries. It is abundantly clear, however, that Musa was neither lacking in self-confidence nor focused on merely short-term occupation. In the same year as the fall of Toledo in 711, he was already minting coins with a Latin inscription proclaiming the Muslim creed, modelled on the Byzantine issues in North Africa: *In nomine Dei Non Deus Nisi Deus Solus Non Deus Alius.* In the Name of God, There is no God but God.

Astonishingly, within five years of their arrival, having taken advantage of the lack of a single, unified adversary on the peninsula, Musa and Tariq had brought the majority of it under Muslim authority. Only the mountainous north-east eluded Muslim rule. There was a clear and present danger, however, in this extraordinary success. Triumphs overseas aroused both pride and envy at the highest level back home. From time to time the most successful commanders, be they in the deserts of North Africa (Uqba ibn Nafi al Fihri) or the burning plains of the Indian Subcontinent (Mohammed ibn al Qasim), found that their glorious, God-given conquests were just as likely to bring about their downfall, and perhaps an unpleasant death,

*previous pages*   In 732 Charles, duke and prince of the Franks, faced an Arab army led by Abd al Rahman al Ghafiq, governor of Al Andalus, at the Battle of Tours. 'In the blink of an eye, they annihilated the Arabs with the sword,' a chronicle reported.

In 651 Yazdgird III was murdered outside the ancient city of Merv, marking the final demise of the Sasanid Empire. In 747 the Abbasids unfurled their black banners here, toppled the Umayyads in 750 and ushered in a new dynasty that would last until 1258.

as phenomenal riches. It was not long before Musa and Tariq received the ominous recall to Damascus. As ever, it was the accession of a new caliph, after the death of Walid in 715, that brought about the reversal. Anxious to please his new Umayyad master Sulayman, Musa took with him some Spanish nobles, large quantities of gold and silver, pearls and precious stones, together with many other gifts including, bizarrely, 'ointments to kindle women's desire'. We may never know the success or otherwise of the aphrodisiacs, but the presents failed to have the desired effect. 'Musa was ignominiously removed from the prince's presence and paraded with a rope around his neck,' the *Chronicle of 754* noted. The great booty he had won in battle was also confiscated. He died around 717, most probably in captivity. There was no justice in this world. His son Abd al Aziz ibn Musa became the first governor of Al Andalus before he was assassinated, supposedly having developed exalted ideas of kingship above his station, in defiance of the more egalitarian Arab traditions.

Monumentally important for the inhabitants of Spain, this westernmost Muslim conquest caused few ripples of interest in the Umayyad heartland. It was remote, far from the imperial capital in Damascus and, initially at least, generated little revenue for the centre.

The highpoint of Arab expansion in the West came in the 720s with repeated forays across the Pyrenees and into the Rhône valley in southern France. These never achieved lasting hold, however, and in 732 nemesis struck. At the Battle of Tours (also known as the Battle of Poitiers), an Arab army led by Abd al Rahman al Ghafiq, governor of Al Andalus, faced Charles, duke and prince of the Franks. During fierce fighting, according to the *Chronicle of 754*, the European army remained 'immobile as a wall' and held together 'like a glacier'. Then, 'In the blink of an eye, they annihilated the Arabs with the sword'. Abd al Rahman was killed, the Christian army victorious. Charles was given the honorific Martellus, the Hammer. Tours sounded the death knell for further Islamic conquests in Europe. Had the Muslims prevailed, Gibbon imagined more than a thousand years later, an Arabian fleet might have sailed unchallenged into the Thames. 'Perhaps the interpretation of the *Koran* would now be taught in the schools of Oxford, and her pulpits might demonstrate to a circumcised people the sanctity and truth of the revelation of Mahomet.'[76]

As it was, the rout at Tours ensured that Oxford students missed out on these opportunities, but Islam sank its roots deep in Spain over the following centuries. Cordoba, Granada and Seville, among other cities, became enormously rich, cosmopolitan and culturally pre-eminent centres, lording it over their Christian counterparts in Europe with élan. The Arab Conquests led to the swift creation of Al Andalus which, in time, became one of the jewels in the Islamic world, a byword for glittering civilization, unity and glory. Its loss during the final chapter of the Reconquista in 1492 was, for the Arabs, nothing less than a calamity.

# Conclusion

The end, when it came, was typically brutal. The Umayyad dynasty had risen swiftly and spectacularly to its world-illuminating, world-conquering zenith. Birthed in blood following the assassination of Ali and Muawiya's ruthless usurpation of power in 661, the Umayyads hurtled towards their own blood-spattered nadir and final destruction in the opening decades of the eighth century.

Eight Umayyad caliphs ruled the Islamic Empire between 715 and 750, a period which witnessed mounting opposition to what increasingly resembled a family business. Too much power and prosperity was centred in one family, the Umayyads' detractors began to murmur. The caliphs Walid, Sulayman (r. 715–17), Hisham (r. 724–43) and Yazid II (r. 720–4) were all sons of Abd al Malik, while Umar II (r. 717–20) and Marwan II (r. 744–50) were his nephews. Muawiya, in the eyes of his numerous critics, had led the move away from a spiritual caliphate, replacing it

Decadent to the end, the last Umayyad caliphs devoted themselves to hunting, music, wine-quaffing and dancing girls in their lavish desert palaces, such as this vast palace-fortress of Qasr al Hayr al Sharqi, near Palmyra.

and abasing it with a dynastic form of 'mere kingship'.[77] He was the first caliph to create a bodyguard, a police force and court chamberlains. He sat on a throne, expropriated property for himself as he saw fit and used slaves on his building projects.

For as long as the morale-boosting military conquests continued unabated, opposition remained muted. Yet the catastrophic failure of a two-year siege of Constantinople during 717–18 represented an unprecedented reversal for the Umayyads. Accustomed to a procession of God-given victories over the infidels, emaciated Arab warriors were reduced instead to a pitiful condition, eating dead animals and scraps of pitch from their ships. A relief mission carrying grain, weapons and supplies was seized and plundered by the Byzantines, bringing an ignominious end to the expedition.

The decadence of the later Umayyad caliphs became increasingly brazen. During Hisham's caliphate Arab armies were kept busy, yet the continual warfare succeeded less in extending the empire's borders than in draining imperial coffers, already hollowed out by the mass conversion to Islam of previously tax-

paying peasants. Hisham was rarely seen in Damascus and, like a number of the later Umayyads, preferred to enjoy himself in his lavish desert palaces – especially the vast palace-fortress of Qasr al Hayr al Sharqi, near Palmyra, a complex of 10 square kilometres where he could enjoy the delights of hunting, music, wine and singing girls.

At least Hisham was lion-hearted on the battlefield. The same could hardly be said of the short-lived caliph Walid II (r. 743–44), who abjectly failed to live up to his more impressive namesake and was instead addicted to hunting, wine, music, poetry and sex, pursuits that were memorably celebrated in the following verse:

> I would that all wine were a dinar a glass
> And all cunts on a lion's brow.
> Then only the liberal would drink
> And only the brave make love.[78]

Walid was widely considered a degenerate and a libertine, a reputation in no way undiminished by his sacrilegious use of a copy of the Quran as a shooting target. Frescoes from his desert palace Qasr Amra in eastern Jordan, one of the earliest surviving examples of Islamic art and architecture, include images of bare-breasted women amid wild scenes of wine-drinking and hunting. Walid's opulent palaces, complete with swimming pools and wine-filled marble baths, were the Playboy Mansions of their day.

While caliphs fiddled, the caliphate burned. Full-blown rebellions burst out in the 740s, starting with the Berbers in North Africa in 740 in a violent and bloody revolt that brought Christians and Kharijite Muslims together in a full-scale challenge to the empire. The year 744 was an *annus horribilis* for the Umayyads. Three caliphs came and went, with a fourth appointed in a desperate bid to stem the chaos. First Walid was overthrown, killed and beheaded. His successor, Yazid III, died less

Scholars at work in a mosque's library, as seen in an Arab miniature from a twelfth-century manuscript by Al Hariri. The Arab Conquests paved the way for the golden age of Islamic culture, presided over by Baghdad for half a millennium.

فقال لهم الجون ارجوا ان يسمع وللصدق وحق بن زبد ان زبد ... يوم لكحيكم لكذ اليوم وقال فكان الجماع

ابن لابسبع وقد واربد تصدر يود دعوتد ما فجرى في افكارهم وفطن لما باطن من ابتسكام وحا اذار

ثم فال اب واه لا بص وشاه القول ابض اطاصه الهوهم ... لهن اثم

الشك وفنل ايهاكم ابن ماذ عبد لاستجان يكم الرجال او باز

than a year into his reign, replaced by Ibrahim, who was in turn almost immediately replaced by Marwan II, whose accession inaugurated the third *fitna* or civil war. In 746 a rebel in Yemen declared himself caliph and seized Mecca and Medina before he was killed in 748. A far more serious Shia revolution had been smouldering in southern Iraq from 719, when enemies of the Umayyads in the holy city of Kufa sent a messenger disguised as a perfume-seller to a village south of the Dead Sea in Jordan. His mission was to encourage a distant descendant of the Prophet Mohammed's family to champion a rebellion against the hated regime. Abu al Abbas, great-great-grandson of the Prophet's uncle Abbas, became the moral leader of the movement. Though their blood ties with the Prophet were more distant than those of the House of Ali, the Abbasids' powers of organization, and the ruthlessness of Abu al Abbas, were unequalled. Growing numbers of the Shia felt alienated by the corrupt Sunni clan in Damascus who had stolen the caliphate from its rightful owners, while the puritanical Kharijites detected sin everywhere and were in revolt.

On 15 June 747, the hitherto clandestine insurgents unfurled their black banners for the first time on the outskirts of Merv. Thousands flocked to take up arms in a great coalition of Shia, Khorasanian and Abbasid forces. By 748, the Abbasids had taken Merv under their military leader Abu Muslim, victorious in a string of battles with the Umayyads, infamous for having reputedly killed 60,000 people in cold blood. A year later, Al Abbas was pronounced caliph Al Saffa, 'The Shedder of Blood', in the great mosque at Kufa.

In January 750, Marwan's Umayyad forces faced the Abbasid rebels on the banks of the Great Zab River, a tributary of the Tigris in northern Iraq. The imperial army, which the tenth-century chronicler Theophanes estimated at 300,000, massively outnumbered the men with black banners. Marwan's cavalry charged confidently, but failed to penetrate the Abbasid wall of lances. Many were impaled on the spot, many others deserted and huge numbers drowned in the foaming waters. It was a complete rout. Damascus fell in April amid fierce fighting between Umayyads and Abbasids and possibly within Umayyad ranks. Theophilus of Edessa, the eighth-century Greek chronicler, reported indescribable scenes of bloodshed as the former imperial capital was ransacked.

The Abbasids 'spent three hours lopping heads in the markets, streets and houses, and they seized their money... Al Walid was amongst those killed, and on that day a great number of Jews and Christians were killed.'[79] Throats were slit, heads were cut off, Umayyads were disinterred and burned. The city's great buildings were sacked, its defences destroyed and royal tombs profaned. Some reports claimed the Abbasids even ploughed up the cemetery in which the martyrs of the siege of Damascus in 634, including the Companions of the Prophet, had been buried. The sanguinary destruction was devastating as 'The Blood Shedder' (r. 749–54) glorified in slaughter. The caliph Marwan fled as far as Egypt where he was hunted down and killed while hiding in a church. Umayyad princes were butchered en masse in a concerted and almost entirely successful effort to eliminate the bloodline.[80]

The Umayyad dynasty had been exterminated. Never mind that Muawiya and his successors in short order had carved out an empire that spanned three continents and ranged from the Caucasus in the north to the Indian Subcontinent in the south, from Morocco and Spain in the west to Afghanistan in the east. In a process that the great fourteenth-century historian Ibn Khaldun would later recognize, a warlike dynasty had stormed to prominence, risen to great heights, and had then become corrupt and decadent before plunging into the abyss. For the next five hundred years it would be the black banners of the Abbasids that would fly over the caliphate, now headquartered in Baghdad, the fabled 'Fountainhead of Scholars'. The era of the Great Arab Conquests was over.

*

The legacy of those conquests changed the world forever. Fourteen centuries later, almost two billion men, women and children, a quarter of the world's population, experience it in their daily lives, from births, deaths and marriages (not to mention divorces and circumcisions) to all manner of religious rituals and traditions, prayers and pilgrimages, politics, cooking and cuisine, banking and business, reading, writing and communicating, art, architecture, literature, music, culture – and civilization writ large.

*Bismillah al Rahman al Rahim*, In the Name of God the Most Gracious the Most Merciful, says the preacher, the president, the poet, the newsreader, the teacher, the businessman, before launching into the business of the day, be it a sermon or a speech, a press conference, public reading, news programme, general announcement or meeting. *Bismillah*, says every Arabic-speaking man, woman and child on the planet before tucking into breakfast, lunch or dinner. *Alhamdulillah*, thank God, Arabic speakers exclaim in one of the most widely used expressions on earth, giving thanks to the Almighty for anything and everything under the sun. Even the future belongs to the divine, and is always governed by the omnipresent *inshallah*, God willing, for who, apart from Allah, knows what will happen in an hour, tomorrow, next week, or next year?

The conquering Arabs brought Arabic and Islam to the world. The consequences of the conquests were unquestionably profound, though they were not necessarily immediate. Beyond the short-term shock of surrender or slaughter for a particular province or community, beyond the negotiations or bloodshed and killing, it took time for their more lasting effects to sink in.

Islam, as we understand it today, was still a work and faith in progress in 750. Though the Quran had been compiled into a book during the caliphate of Abu Bakr, the great intellectual underpinnings of the faith – such as the four schools of Sunni Islam, the emergence of a powerful class of religious scholars generating vast reams of Islamic jurisprudence, together with the *Sunna* (social and legal traditions), the *hadith* (sayings of the Prophet), Quranic exegesis, and diverse matters doctrinal, theological and philosophical – were either in their infancy or had yet to emerge. The gathering and codification of the Prophet's sayings, for example, was in its earliest stages. As a Muslim scholar wrote around 740, 'I never heard Jabir ibn Zayd [theologian, d. c. 720] say: "The prophet said..." and yet the young men round here are saying it twenty times an hour.'[81] Islam's intellectual ballast would be laid down in earnest over the following centuries, above all during the first half of the Abbasid half millennium beginning in 750.

In time, ambitious local dynasties and opportunist upstarts would tear down the political unity of the vast caliphate which the Umayyads had extended to its widest frontiers. Such union has proved vanishingly elusive ever since, the stuff of haunting dreams for many Arabs from Egypt's Pan-Arabist Gamal Abdel Nasser to today's jihadists hell-bent on restoring the caliphate. One might argue that the Arab Conquests planted the seeds of the Muslim superiority complex as the last of the three Abrahamic revealed religions while, for a tiny minority of the faithful, one of the more baleful legacies over the centuries has been the enduring attraction of holy war against the 'infidels'. Yet though this sort of highly idealized caliphate or single statehood has never reappeared, Muslims could always draw strength from their spiritual unity as part of the greater *ummah*, a heartfelt reality which survives for Muslim 'brothers' and 'sisters' to this day. Relatively minor theological differences might divide a

Sunni Muslim from a Shia, but in the final analysis both were, and still are, Muslim, adherents of the same faith. Both subscribe to the common creed: *la ilaha illa Allah, Mohammedun rasul Allah*, there is no God but God, Mohammed is His prophet.[82] It is a remarkable fact, too, that the overwhelming majority of the territories conquered by the Arabs in the seventh and eighth centuries remain Muslim today, with the obvious exception of the Iberian Peninsula. And it is no less notable that over the following centuries the faith only grew and grew from its earliest beginnings, in lands far beyond the scope of those conquests and this book, more through the power of spiritual and cultural attraction – as well as the financial incentives to convert – than the steel of an Arab sword.

Faith was not the only thing that united Arabs – over time – with most of the peoples they conquered. The tongue of the Arab conquerors was Arabic, which from the outset became the totem of the ruling elite. Thanks to Arabian traders, Arabic was already known in much of the conquered territory, above all in Syria and Iraq, but the use of the language by the all-conquering new masters, as opposed to the politically marginal merchants, lifted it onto a new plane entirely. The ruling class in Byzantine provinces in Syria and Iraq were largely Greek speakers, while the Sasanian elite spoke mainly Persian. Arabic, the language of the conquerors, the language of the state as well as the language of God as revealed to the Prophet Mohammed in the Quran, steadily advanced, displacing or eclipsing Greek, Persian, Coptic and Aramaic, among other languages. This was by no means uniform across the caliphate, as evidenced today in the contrast between Muslim Iran, where Farsi remains the dominant tongue, and Egypt, where Arabic took root over several centuries and where it now holds sway among Muslims and Coptic Christians alike.[83] The numerous local dialects may differ from one Arab country to another, so that a Moroccan and a Saudi meeting for the first time might have no idea what the other is talking about, but the 'rich, strange, subtle, suavely hypnotic, magically persuasive, maddeningly difficult' classical Arabic remains the greatest unifier.[84]

The Arab Conquests were the midwife for the birth of a glorious new civilization, heir to both Rome and Persia. Having united an extraordinarily large landmass under the banner of Islamic rule, they set the stage for the Dar al Islam's riposte to the Golden Age of Greece. 'Seek knowledge even to China', ran one of the famous *hadiths*, and the Arabs took the Prophet at his word.

Under the Abbasids of Baghdad, the Islamic world built on its rich inheritance from the Umayyads and became tolerant, pluralist, cosmopolitan, culturally rich, outward-looking and intellectually inquisitive, a trailblazer for new discoveries in which Jews and Christians, among many other communities, played an integral role. In a whirlwind of cultural development beginning in the late eighth century under the charismatic caliph Harun al Rashid, star of *The Arabian Nights*, Islamic civilization became the greatest and most sophisticated on earth. Landmark works of classical Greek, Persian and Hindu scholarship were translated into Arabic, revised, developed and improved, before being circulated around the Islamic Empire and far beyond. From Plato and Aristotle to Euclid and Hippocrates, knowledge passed from West to East and, through deep-pocketed Arab patronage, survived to pass back, centuries later, into Western civilization. Arab scientists, mathematicians, musicians, writers and poets, physicians, historians, philosophers, astronomers, legalists and lexicographers all beat a path to Baghdad and joined a cultural revolution that was every bit as remarkable as the conquests which had laid the foundations for it.

We may wonder, all these centuries later, how relatively small numbers of Arab warriors could topple one once mighty empire, shatter a second and build a world-spanning empire

طبقه اخرى لا يغشيها بغلاف لها إلا إنها لما بلغت اقبضقوة لحم الملتحم من ابها
غتأتلتم حول الطبقه القرنيه ودعته يغشيها بها يغشي سائر الطبقات بعضها
بعضها بعضا لانه لو غشاه كله لمنع البصر من ان يبصر ه
وهو على هذا المثال

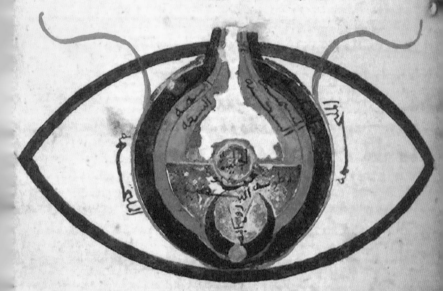

واستدى بالاخبار عن منافع كل واحد من الرطوبات والطبقات التي وصفنا مع
ابتدا اثبانها وكونها ومنتها وموضعها وتركبته تقدمت من اخبارك
ان الرطوبه الجليديه في وسط البصر وان خلفها رطوبه واحده وثلث طبقا
وقدامها رطوبه واحده وثلث طبقات ه فنبتدى بعون الله بالاخبار
عن منفعه الرطوبه التي خلف الجليديه وهو الزجاجيه وعن الثلث
طبقات التي ذكرنا خلفها فنقول ان كل عضو من اعضا البدن لابد له من غذا

of their own in the matter of a few decades, while introducing a new faith whose rise would be scarcely less astonishing than these phenomenal territorial gains. Unquestionably it helped that the Arabs chose to launch themselves upon the world in the immediate aftermath of the Byzantine–Sasanian War, during which the two old foes had battered themselves to destruction for an entire generation. Surging out of the pitiless peninsula, the Arab horsemen found themselves quite literally in the right place at the right time. It helped, too, that the faith they carried with them was far less novel and radical than it might appear to non-Muslims today. Given Islam's lifting of the core features from the earlier Abrahamic religions, the 'new' creed could be marketed compellingly and convincingly as a return to the true faith from which believers had strayed. And by definition, unlike Judaism especially, Islam was inherently inclusive. Conversion to the faith of the conquerors could be the matter of a few words in as many seconds. Islam, in other words, contained a built-in mechanism for expansion. It is difficult to imagine its subsequent global success without this defining, open-to-all feature. The reassuring familiarity of Islam, combined with the ease with which new believers could convert to it, proved just as important to the conquests as outright military might.

Ultimately the faith-filled Arab warriors lived up to their self-appointed, world-conquering role with élan. They considered themselves irresistible, their mission divinely sanctioned. As success followed success with stunning speed and regularity during the extraordinary 120 years that followed the Prophet Mohammed's death, the sacred smash-and-grab operation turned into something far greater, at once epoch-making and imperial on the grandest scale. Even the Arabs' most steadfast enemies must have wondered whether this was indeed God's destiny for humankind.

An anatomical drawing of the human eye by Hunayn ibn Ishaq (808–73), doyen of Abbasid scientists and chief translator in Abbasid Baghdad's House of Wisdom. Hunayn's *Ten Treatises on the Eye* is considered the first systematic textbook of ophthalmology.

# Appendix

*Timeline of Key Dates*

*A selection of passages
from key primary sources for
the Arab Conquests*

**c.570**
Birth of the Prophet Mohammed.

**c.600**
Birth of Muawiya, the future Umayyad caliph.

**602**
Khosrow II, the Sasanian King of Kings, launches his war against the Byzantines in the aftermath of the murder of the emperor Maurice.

**610**
Mohammed receives his first divine revelation in a mountain cave above Mecca.

**613**
Mohammed starts to preach his revelations from God.

**612**
Damascus falls to Khosrow II.

**614**
Jerusalem falls.

**617**
Khosrow invades Egypt.

**619**
The Persians conquer Anatolia and Egypt.

**622**
The *hijra*: Mohammed migrates with his followers from Mecca to Medina.

**624**
Mohammed leads the first Muslim army in history to victory at the Battle of Badr.

**625**
Mohammed expels the Jewish Nadir tribe from Medina. They follow the Qaynuqa into exile after being accused of plotting to assassinate the Prophet.

**627**
Mohammed and his Muslims defeat the Meccans at the Battle of Al Khandaq (The Trench). Between 600 and 800 Jews, accused of plotting against the Prophet, are executed.

In a devastating Byzantine counter-attack, Heraclius routs the Persians at Nineveh.

**628**
Yavad II, son of Khosrow II, over-throws his father in a coup and has him murdered, ushering in a period of severe instability.

The new Persian king offers favourable terms to the Byzantine emperor Heraclius. The Byzantine–Sasanian War ends. Both empires are exhausted and return to the *status quo ante bellum*.

**630**
Mecca surrenders to Mohammed. It becomes the first Muslim conquest.

The distinguished Persian general Shahrbaraz launches a coup, the first person from outside the royal dynasty in four centuries to attempt to seize the throne.

Heraclius becomes the first Byzantine emperor to visit the Holy City, returning the relics of the True Cross, restored from Persian capture, to Jerusalem.

## 632

Death of Mohammed. Abu Bakr becomes caliph.

At the age of eight, Yazdgird III ascends to the Persian throne, inheriting an empire in chaos.

## 632–3

Ridda Wars break out across the Arabian Peninsula. The rebels who rose up against Abu Bakr are defeated in a series of campaigns.

## 633

An Arab army is marauding in Iraq, prelude to a full-blown invasion.

Hira becomes the first Iraqi city to pay tribute to the conquerors.

## 634

Damascus falls to the Arab Muslims, the first major Byzantine trophy.

Death of Abu Bakr. Umar ibn al Khattab becomes caliph.

An Arab army under Abu Ubayd is defeated at the Battle of the Bridge.

## c.635

Battle of Qadisiyya. In a landmark victory the Arab army led by Saad ibn Abi Waqqas crushes Rustam Farrokhzad's Persians, delivering a fatal blow to the Sasanian Empire.

## 636

Battle of Yarmuk. The Arab commander Khalid ibn Walid defeats Heraclius. Christian rule in Syria ends.

## 637

Sophronius, Patriarch of Jerusalem, surrenders the Holy City to the caliph Umar.

The Syrian city of Homs falls to the conquerors.

A Persian army makes its last stand against the Arabs at Jalula and is defeated.

## 638

Susa falls to Abu Musa's Arab forces.

## 639

The Arab general Amr ibn al As invades Egypt with a Muslim army.

Umar appoints Muawiya governor of Syria.

640

The Egyptian city of Babylon falls.

Alexandria surrenders with barely a fight.

## 641

Death of the emperor Heraclius. Amr ibn al As routs the Byzantines at Misr al Fustat, the site of the future city of Cairo.

**642**
Battle of Nihavand. The Arabs defeat Yazdgird III's Persian army in the 'Victory of Victories', which triggers the disintegration of the Sasanian Empire.

**644**
Assassination of Umar. Uthman ibn Affan becomes caliph.
Tripoli is the last Byzantine city to fall, bringing Christian rule along the eastern Mediterranean to a close.

**647**
An Arab army defeats the Byzantines at Sbeitla in southern Tunisia, the only major engagement between the two sides in North Africa.

**648**
Muawiya assembles the first-ever Muslim fleet, invades Cyprus and imposes a punitive tribute on the island a year later.

**650s**
Conquests begin in Afghanistan.

**651**
Murder of Yazdgird III at Merv.
The death of the king heralds the end of the Sasanian Empire.

**c.653**
Muawiya appoints Habib ibn Maslama to command his Syrian forces in a triumphant campaign against Armenia. The Byzantine commander Maurianos is defeated and killed.

**654**
Muawiya occupies Rhodes.

**655**
The Battle of the Masts. A Muslim fleet under Muawiya's command routs the Byzantines off the Antalyan port town of Finike in southwest Turkey. The victory over a large Christian fleet personally commanded by the emperor Constans II establishes, for the first time, Muslim naval supremacy in the eastern Mediterranean.

**656**
Assassination of Uthman by Muslim rebels. Ali ibn Abi Talib, son-in-law and cousin of the Prophet Mohammed, becomes caliph.
The killing of Uthman and the rise of Ali as caliph usher in the First Fitna, or Civil War, between Muslims.
The Battle of the Camel, the first major conflict between Muslims. Ali is victorious over an army partly led by the Prophet Mohammed's widow Aisha.

**657**
Battle of Siffin. Muawiya takes to the field against Ali in an inconclusive encounter.

**660**
Muawiya declares himself caliph.

**661**
Assassination of Ali. Muawiya becomes caliph. First Fitna ends when Ali's son and heir Hasan ibn Ali acknowledges Muawiya's authority. Umayyad dynasty is founded, headquartered in Damascus.

**664**
Muawiya snuffs out the Kharijite rebellion against his authority.

**668**
Muawiya's army reaches Chalcedon and puts Constantinople under siege. The city successfully resists.

**670**
Muawiya appoints Uqba ibn Nafi al Fihri governor of Muslim lands in North Africa.
Uqba founds the city of Qairouan, prelude to a series of raids and conquests reaching as far west as the Atlantic.

**674**
Muawiya launches a second, unsuccessful attempt to take Constantinople.

**680**
Death of Muawiya. His son and heir Yazid I becomes caliph.
Battle of Karbala. A small army led by the former caliph Ali's son Husayn, grandson of the Prophet, is defeated by Umayyad forces loyal to Yazid. Husayn is martyred and beheaded.
Second Fitna begins for control of the Islamic Empire.

**682**
Uqba is killed in battle in Algeria.

**685**
Abd al Malik becomes caliph.

**692**
Siege of Mecca. A Syrian army of seven thousand crushes and kills the rebel and self-proclaimed 'caliph' Abdullah ibn al Zubayr. End of Second Fitna.

**694**
The caliph Abd al Malik appoints Al Hajjaj ibn Yusuf al Thaqafi governor of Iraq and the eastern lands.

**696**
Al Hajjaj quashes another Kharijite rebellion in Iraq.

**698**
Al Hajjaj appoints Ubayd Allah ibn Abi Bakra to lead the 'Army of Destruction' against the recalcitrant Zunbil dynasty of southern Afghanistan.
Arabs capture Carthage.

**705**
Death of Abd al Malik. Al Walid becomes caliph.
Qutayba ibn Muslim is promoted governor of Khorasan.

**706**
Abd al Malik builds the peerless Umayyad Mosque in Damascus at a reported cost of 600,000–1,000,000 dinars.

**708**
Arabs capture Tangiers.

**709**
The northern Afghan city of Balkh falls to the Umayyads.

The city of Bukhara (Uzbekistan) falls.

**711**
Tariq ibn Ziyad, a Berber commander, crosses the Straits of Gibraltar with Muslim forces and lands on the Iberian Peninsula.

Battle of Guadelete. Tariq defeats the Visigothic king Roderic in the first clash between Muslims and Christians in present-day Spain.

Cordoba and Toledo fall to the Muslims.

**712**
Musa ibn Nusayr, the newly appointed Arab governor of Ifriqiya, crosses the Straits of Gibraltar with a second Muslim army.
Samarkand falls finally to the Arabs.

**713**
An Arab delegation arrives in the Tang court of China.

**714**
Death of Al Hajjaj.

**715**
Death of Al Walid. Sulayman becomes caliph.

**717**
Death of the commander Musa ibn Nusayr, probably in captivity.

**717–8**
A two-year Arab siege of Constantinople fails catastrophically.

**720s**
Highpoint of Arab expansion in the West. Repeated forays across the Pyrenees and into the Rhône valley in southern France.

**726**
Khazars kill the Arab governor of Armenia.

**732**
Battle of Tours. An Arab army led by Abd al Rahman al Ghafiq, governor of Al Andalus, is routed by Charles, duke and prince of the Franks. Abd al Rahman is killed.

**740s**
Full-blown rebellions burst out, starting with the Berbers in North Africa in 740 in a violent and bloody revolt that brings Christians and Kharijite Muslims together in a full-scale challenge to the empire.

**744**
Three caliphs come and go. Marwan II becomes the last Umayyad caliph.

Third Fitna breaks out as Umayyad authority begins to splinter.

**746**
A rebel in Yemen seizes Mecca and Medina and declares himself caliph. He is killed in 748.

**747**
Abbasid revolution begins outside Merv.

**748**
Merv falls to the Abbasid general Abu Muslim.

**749**
Al Abbas is pronounced caliph Al Saffa, 'The Shedder of Blood', in the great mosque at Kufa in southern Iraq.

**750**
Battle of the Great Zab River. The Abbasids trounce Marwan's Umayyad forces.

Damascus falls. The Umayyads are slaughtered. The dynasty is finished.

**751**
Battle of Talas. An Abbasid Arab army, supported by Tibetan allies and Turks, defeats Tang Chinese forces and reasserts Muslim control over Transoxiana.

**754**
Death of Al Saffa. Al Mansur 'The Victorious' becomes caliph.

**755**
Abd al Rahman, sole royal Umayyad survivor of the massacre in Damascus, lands on the Iberian Peninsula after dodging assassins for five years. He founds the amirate of Cordoba in 756.

**762**
Mansur begins work on his new capital, Baghdad. Work is completed in 766. The city remains the head-quarters of the Islamic caliphate until 1258. For much of that time it is the greatest city on earth, showcase of the world-beating Islamic Empire.

## Appendix
## 1. Al Baladhuri on the Battle of Yarmuk, 636

Al Baladhuri was an eminent ninth-century historian, whose *Kitab Futuh al Buldun* (*'Book of the Conquests of Lands'*) was considered the definitive account of this period for centuries. Here he writes about the fateful Battle of Yarmuk in 636, an Arab victory that brought Christian rule in Syria to a bloody and catastrophic end.

*A description of the battle.*

Heraclius gathered large bodies of Greeks, Syrians, Mesopotamians and Armenians numbering about 200,000. This army he put under the command of one of his choice men and sent as a vanguard Jabalah ibn al Aiham al Ghassani at the head of the 'naturalized' Arabs [*mustaaribah*] of Syria of the tribes of Lakhm, Judham and others, resolving to fight the Muslims so that he might either win or withdraw to the land of the Greeks and live in Constantinople. The Muslims gathered together and the Greek army marched against them. The battle they fought at Al Yarmuk was of the fiercest and bloodiest kind. Al Yarmuk [Hieromax] is a river. In this battle 24,000 Muslims took part. The Greeks and their followers in this battle tied themselves to each other by chains, so that no one might set his hope on flight. By Allah's help, some 70,000 of them were put to death, and their remnants took to flight, reaching as far as Palestine, Antioch, Aleppo, Mesopotamia and Armenia. In the Battle of Al Yarmuk certain Muslim women took part and fought violently. Among them was Hind, daughter of Utba and mother of Muawiya ibn Sufyan, who repeatedly exclaimed, 'Cut the arms of these "uncircumcised", with your swords!' Her husband Abu Sufyan had come to Syria as a volunteer desiring to see his sons, and so he brought his wife with him. He then returned to Al Madinah where he died, year 31, at the age of 88. Others say he died in Syria. When the news of his death was carried to his daughter, Umm Habiba, she waited until the third day on which she ordered some yellow paint and covered with it her arms and face saying, 'I would not have done that, had I not heard the Prophet say, "A woman should not be in mourning for more than three days over anyone except her husband."' It is stated that she did likewise when she received the news of her brother Yazid's death. But Allah knows best.

*Those who lost an eye or suffered martyrdom.* Abu Sufyan ibn Harb was one-eyed. He had lost his eye in the Battle of Al Taif. In the Battle of Al Yarmuk, however, Al Ashaath ibn Qais, Hashim ibn Utba ibn Abi Waqqas al Zuhri (i.e., al-Mirkal) and Qais ibn Makshuh, each lost an eye. In this battle Amir ibn Abi Waqqas Al Zuhri fell a martyr. It is this Amir who once carried the letter of Umar ibn al Khattab assigning Abu Ubaida to the governorship of Syria. Others say he was a victim of the plague; still others report that he suffered martyrdom in the Battle of Ajnadin; but all that is not true.

*Habib ibn Maslama pursues the fugitives.* Abu Ubaida put Habib ibn Maslama al Fihri at the head of a cavalry detachment charged with pursuing the fugitive enemy, and Habib set out killing every man whom he could reach.

…

*Heraclius's adieu to Syria.* When Heraclius received the news about the troops in Al Yarmuk and the destruction of his army by the Muslims, he fled from Antioch to Constantinople, and as he passed Al Daarb he turned and said, 'Peace unto thee, O Syria, and what an excellent country this is for the enemy!' – referring to the numerous pastures in Syria.

The Battle of Al Yarmuk took place in Rajah, year 15.

...

*Christians and Jews prefer Muslim rule.* Abu Hafs al Dimashqi from Said ibn Abd al Aziz: When Heraclius massed his troops against the Muslims and the Muslims heard that they were coming to meet them at Al Yarmuk, the Muslims refunded to the inhabitants of Hims the *kharaj* [tribute] they had taken from them saying, 'We are too busy to support and protect you. Take care of yourselves.' But the people of Hims replied, 'We like your rule and justice far better than the state of oppression and tyranny in which we were. The army of Heraclius we shall indeed, with your "amil's" help, repulse from the city.' The Jews rose and said, 'We swear by the Torah, no governor of Heraclius shall enter the city of Hims unless we are first vanquished and exhausted!' Saying this, they closed the gates of the city and guarded them. The inhabitants of the other cities – Christian and Jew – that had capitulated to the Muslims, did the same, saying, 'If Heraclius and his followers win over the Muslims we would return to our previous condition, otherwise we shall retain our present state so long as numbers are with the Muslims.' When by Allah's help the 'unbelievers' were defeated and the Muslims won, they opened the gates of their cities, went out with the singers and music players who began to play, and paid the kharaj.

Source: *The Origins of the Islamic State, being a translation from the Arabic, accompanied with annotations, geographic and historic notes of the Kitâb fitûh al-buldân of al-Imâm abu-l Abbâs Ahmad ibn-Jâbir al-Balâd-huri, by P. K. Hitti*, (New York, 1916), Volume 1, pp. 207–211.

**Appendix**
**2. The Pact of Umar**

When the Arabs captured new cities from the Byzantines during the early years of the conquests, they struck deals granting the conquered peoples security for their lives, property and places of worship. In return the *dhimmi*, or protected population, were subject to a number of regulations governing many aspects of their lives. Such arrangements, codified into treaties written in Arabic, appear to have originated in around 637 under the new caliph Umar during the conquest of Syria and Palestine, though scholars differ on the dating and authenticity of such a treaty. There are multiple variations of this pact and the text below may be seen as an illustrative version – applying to both Christians and Jews. The text makes no reference to one of the most important tenets governing relations between Muslims and the 'people of the book': the requirement for both Jews and Christians to pay a head-tax in return for their protection, together with their exemption from military service.

*In the name of God, the Merciful, the Compassionate!*
This is a writing to Umar from the Christians of such and such a city. When You [Muslims] marched against us [Christians], we asked of you protection for ourselves, our posterity, our possessions, and our co-religionists; and we made this stipulation with you, that we will not erect in our city or the suburbs any new monastery, church, cell or hermitage; that we will not repair any of such buildings that may fall into ruins, or renew those that may be situated in the Muslim quarters of the town; that we will not refuse the Muslims entry into our churches either by night or by day; that we will open the gates wide to passengers and travellers; that we will receive any Muslim traveller into our houses and give

him food and lodging for three nights; that we will not harbour any spy in our churches or houses, or conceal any enemy of the Muslims. [At least six of these laws were taken over from earlier Christian laws against infidels.]

That we will not teach our children the Quran [some nationalist Arabs feared the infidels would ridicule the Quran; others did not want infidels even to learn the language]; that we will not make a show of the Christian religion nor invite any one to embrace it; that we will not prevent any of our kinsmen from embracing Islam, if they so desire. That we will honour the Muslims and rise up in our assemblies when they wish to take their seats; that we will not imitate them in our dress, either in the cap, turban, sandals, or parting of the hair; that we will not make use of their expressions of speech, nor adopt their surnames [infidels must not use greetings and special phrases employed only by Muslims]; that we will not ride on saddles, or gird on swords, or take to ourselves arms or wear them, or engrave Arabic inscriptions on our rings; that we will not sell wine [forbidden to Muslims]; that we will shave the front of our heads; that we will keep to our own style of dress, wherever we may be; that we will wear girdles round our waists [infidels wore leather or cord girdles; Muslims, cloth and silk].

That we will not display the cross upon our churches or display our crosses or our sacred books in the streets of the Muslims, or in their market-places; that we will strike the clappers in our churches lightly [wooden rattles or bells summoned the people to church or synagogue]; that we will not recite our services in a loud voice when a Muslim is present; that we will not carry Palm branches [on Palm Sunday] or our images in procession in the streets; that at the burial of our dead we will not chant loudly or carry lighted candles in the streets of the Muslims or their market places; that we will not take any slaves that have already been in the possession of Muslims, nor spy into their houses; and that we will not strike any Muslim.

All this we promise to observe, on behalf of ourselves and our co-religionists, and receive protection from you in exchange; and if we violate any of the conditions of this agreement, then we forfeit your protection and you are at liberty to treat us as enemies and rebels.

Source: Jacob Marcus, *The Jew in the Medieval World: A Sourcebook*, 315–1791 (New York, 1938), pp. 13–15.

Appendix
3. Al Tabari on the royal booty seized in the aftermath of the
fall of Madain, 637

No history of early Islam and the Arab Conquests can be understood without reference to the ninth-century author Mohammed
ibn Jarir al Tabari, foremost among Arab historians. His thirty-
nine volume *History of the Prophets and Kings* is genuinely
monumental – in English it runs to 10,000 pages – and covers
the conquests with extraordinary insight and captivating detail.

The extract below vividly illustrates one of their most powerful
and enduring motivations: the lure of booty. It describes the
aftermath of the Battle of Qadisiyya and the capture of Al Madain,
with the defeated Persian army in headlong flight, energetically
pursued by Saad ibn Abi Waqqas, the Arab commander, and his
booty-hunting warriors.

*Mention of the Booty Amassed from the People of Al Madain*

They said: When Saad entered Al Madain, he saw that it was
vacated. Finally, he came to the Great Hall of the king's palace
and started to recite, 'How many gardens and springs (flowing
therein) have they abandoned, how many sown fields and noble habitats, how many comforts in which they took delight! The
situation was thus. We bequeathed them (and their properties)
to another people.' Then he performed a prayer ritual commem-
orating the conquest; this was no congregational prayer meeting.
He performed eight *rakaas* [Islamic prayer movements] without
pauses between them. He adopted the Great Hall as site for the
prayer ritual. There were plaster statues there, of men and horses,
but that did not prevent Saad, nor the other Muslims, (from praying there) and they were left as they were.

They said: Saad performed the prayer ritual on the day he
entered the city; that was because he intended to stay there for

the time being. The first Friday prayer ritual held in Iraq was the one held in congregation in Al Madain in Safar of the year 16 (March 637).

According to Al Sari Shuayb Sayf Mohammed, Al Muhallab, Uqba, Amr, Abu Umar and Said: Saad settled in the Great Hall of the King and dispatched Zuhrah with the order to go straight away to Al Nahrawan. In addition, he sent similar detachments in every direction to expel the unbelievers and collect the spoils. After three days he moved to the palace. He entrusted Amr ibn Amr ibn Mugarrin with control over what was confiscated and ordered him to collect what was in the palace, the Great Hall and the private compounds. He also had to count what the search parties had produced. The inhabitants of Al Madain, at the time of the defeat, had quickly snatched up what they could before fleeing in every direction. Not one of them, however, escaped with anything that did not eventually turn up in the camp of Mihran at Al Nahrawan; not even a piece of string. The search parties chased after them to the extent that they retrieved everything that those fleeing had taken with them; the Muslims brought back what the latter had snatched up in order to add all that to what already had been amassed. The first objects to be collected on that day were from the White Palace, the living quarters of the king and the other compounds of Al Madain.

According to Al Sari Shuayb Sayf al Aamash Habib ibn Suhban: We marched into Al Madain and came upon Turkish tents filled with baskets sealed with leaden seals. At first, we did not think they would contain anything but food, but later they were found to contain vessels of gold and silver. These were later distributed among the men. At the time, Habib (ibn Suhban) went on, I saw a man running around shouting, 'Who has silver or gold in his possession?' We also came upon large quantities of camphor which we mistook for salt. So we began to knead it (in our dough) until we discovered that it made our bread taste bitter.

According to Al Sari Shuayb Sayf al Nadr ibn al Sari ibn al Rufayl – his father Al Rufayl ibn Maysur: Zuhrah left with his vanguard, ordering them to follow him. Finally, they came to the bridge at Al Nahrawan. The Persians were actually on it, packed together. Suddenly a mule fell into the water. With great effort, the Persians hastened to retrieve it. Zuhrah exclaimed, 'I swear by God, there must be something important about that mule. They would not have put in so much effort to retrieve it, nor would they have endured our swords in this dangerous situation, unless there was something special they did not want to give up.'And sure enough, on this mule were packed the king's finery, his clothes, gems, swordbelt and coat of mail encrusted with jewellery. The king used to don all these when sitting in state. Then Zuhrah dismounted to fight. Thereupon, after he had routed them, he ordered his men to retrieve the mule. They lifted it (out of the water) and brought its baggage. Zuhrah returned this to the spoils, he and his men still unaware of its contents. On that day Zuhrah recited the following verses in *rajaz* [a metre used in classical Arabic poetry]:

> My uncles be ransom today for my fighters,
> Recoiling from leaving me there at the river.
> They cleft for (the prize of) the mule in the struggle
> With every sword blow the cranial sutures.
> The Persians were slain covering their own hillocks,
> As if they were (nothing but mere) heads of cattle.

Source: *The History of al-Tabari, Vol. XIII, The Conquest of Iraq, Southwestern Persia, and Egypt*, pp. 23–25.

# Appendix
## 4. Ibn Abd al Hakam on the conquest of Spain, 711

The Arab invasion of Spain, the future Al Andalus, was a landmark in the history of the conquests, thrusting the new Islamic civilization decisively into the heart of Europe. Although the reversal at Tours in 732 marked the highpoint of Islamic incursions in the West, parts of Spain would remain Muslim until the final chapter of the Reconquista in 1492.

The historian Ibn Abd al Hakam was born in Misr al Fustat, the precursor to Cairo, in 803. Freely mixing fact with fiction – or, more politely, tradition – his *Futuh Misr wa'l Maghreb wa'l Andalus* (*Conquest of Egypt, North Africa and Spain*) was one of the earliest Arab Muslim histories. The extract below, which includes a questionable instance of simulated cannibalism, describes Tariq ibn Ziyad's invasion across the Straits of Gibraltar in 711, followed by the Arabs' lightning conquests and plunder.

Musa ibn Nusayr sent his son Marwan to Tangiers, to wage a holy war upon her coast. Having, then, exerted himself together with his friends, he returned, leaving to Tariq ibn Amru the command of his army which amounted to 1,700. Others say that 12,000 Berbers besides 16 Arabs were with Tariq: but that is false. It is also said that Musa ibn Nusayr marched out of Ifriqiya upon an expedition into Tangiers, and that he was the first governor who entered Tangiers, where parts of the Berber tribes Botr and Beranes resided. These had not yet submitted themselves. When he approached Tangiers, he scattered his light troops. On the arrival of his cavalry in the nearest province of Sus, he subdued its inhabitants, and made them prisoners, they yielding him obedience. And he gave them a governor whose conduct was agreeable to them. He sent Ibn Beshr ibn Abi Artah to a citadel, three days' journey from the town of Qairouan. Having taken the former, he made prisoners of the children, and plundered the treasury. The citadel was called Beshr, by which name it is known to this day. Afterwards Musa deposed the viceroy whom he had placed over Tangiers, and appointed Tariq ibn Ziyad governor. He, then, returned to Qairouan, Tariq with his female slave of the name Umm-Hakim setting out for Tangiers. Tariq remained some time in this district, waging a holy war. This was in the year 92. The governor of the straits between this district and Andalus was a foreigner called Ilyan, Lord of Sebta [Ceuta]. He was also the governor of a town called Alchadra, situated on the same side of the straits of Andalus as Tangiers. Ilyan was a subject of Roderic, the Lord of Andalus [i.e. king of Spain], who used to reside in Toledo. Tariq put himself in communication with Ilyan, and treated him kindly, until they made peace with each other. Ilyan had sent one of his daughters to Roderic, the Lord of Andalus, for her improvement and education; but she became pregnant by him. Ilyan having heard of this, said, I see for him no other punishment or recompense, than that I should bring the Arabs against him. He sent to Tariq, saying, I will bring thee to Andalus; Tariq being at that time in Tlemcen, and Musa ibn Nusayr in Qairouan. But Tariq said I cannot trust thee until thou send me a hostage. So he sent his two daughters, having no other children. Tariq allowed them to remain in Tlemcen, guarding them closely. After that Tariq went to Ilyan who was in Sebta on the straits. The latter rejoicing at his coming, said, I will bring thee to Andalus. But there was a mountain called the mountain of Tariq between the two landing places, that is, between Sebta and Andalus. When the evening came, Ilyan brought him the vessels, in which he made him embark for that landing-place, where he concealed himself during the day, and in the evening sent back the vessels to bring over the rest of his companions. So they embarked for the landing-place, none of them being left behind: whereas the people of Andalus did not observe them, thinking that the vessels crossing and recrossing were similar to the trading vessels which for their benefit plied backwards and forwards. Tariq was in the last division which went across. He proceeded to his companions, Ilyan together with the merchants that were with him being left behind in Alchadra, in order that he might the better encourage his companions and countrymen. The news of Tariq and of those who were with him, as well as of the place where they were, reached the people of Andalus. Tariq, going along with his companions, marched over a bridge of mountains to a town called Cartagena. He went in the direction of Cordoba.

Having passed by an island in the sea, he left behind his female slave of the name of Umm-Hakim, and with her a division of his troops. That island was then called Umm-Hakim. When the Muslims settled in the island, they found no other inhabitants there, than vinedressers. They made them prisoners. After that they took one of the vinedressers, slaughtered him, cut him in pieces, and boiled him, while the rest of his companions looked on. They had also boiled meat in other cauldrons. When the meat was cooked, they threw away the flesh of that man which they had boiled; no one knowing that it was thrown away: and they ate the meat which they had boiled, while the rest of the vinedressers were spectators. These did not doubt but that the Muslims ate the flesh of their companion; the rest being afterwards sent away informed the people of Andalus that the Muslims feed on human flesh, acquainting them with what had been done to the vinedresser.

As Abdul Rahman has related to us on the authority of his father Abdallah ibn Abd al Hakam, and of Hisham Ibn Ishaq: There was a house in Andalus, the door of which was secured with padlocks, and on which every new king of the country placed a padlock of his own, until the accession to power of the king against whom the Muslims marched. They therefore begged him to place a padlock on it, as the kings before him were wont to do. But he refused saying, I will place nothing on it, until I shall have known what is inside; he then ordered it to be opened; but behold inside were portraits of the Arabs, and a letter in which it was written: 'When this door shall be opened, these people will invade this country.'

...

When Tariq landed, soldiers from Cordoba came to meet him; and seeing the small number of his companions they despised him on that account. They then fought. The battle with Tariq was severe. They were routed, and he did not cease from the slaughter of them till they reached the town of Cordoba. When Roderic heard of this, he came to their rescue from Toledo. They then fought in a place of the name of Shedunia, in a valley which is called this day the valley of Umm-Hakim [on 11 July 711, at the mouth of the Barbate river]. They fought a severe battle; but God, mighty and great, killed Roderic and his companions. Mugheyth Errumi, a slave of Walid, was then the commander of Tariq's cavalry. Mugheyth Errumi went in the direction of Cordoba, Tariq passing over to Toledo. He, then, entered it, and asked for the table, having nothing else to occupy himself. This, as the men of the Bible relate, was the table of Suleyman ibn Dawud [Solomon], may the blessing of God be upon him.

As Abdul Rahman has related to us on the authority of Yahya ibn Bukeir, and the latter on the authority of Laith ibn Saad: Andalus having been conquered for Musa ibn Nusayr, he took from it the table of Suleyman ibn Dawud, and the crown. Tariq was told that the table was in a citadel called Faras, two days' journey from Toledo, and the governor of this citadel was a nephew of Roderic. Tariq, then, wrote to him, promising safety both for himself and family. The nephew descended from the citadel, and Tariq fulfilled his promise with reference to his safety. Tariq said to him, deliver the table, and he delivered it to him. On this table were gold and silver, the like of which one had not seen. Tariq, then, took off one of its legs together with the pearls and the gold it contained, and fixed to it a similar leg. The table was valued at two hundred thousand dinars, on account of the pearls that were on it. He took up the pearls, the armour, the gold, the silver, and the vases which he had with him, and found that quantity of spoils, the like of which one had not seen. He collected all that. Afterwards he returned to Cordoba, and having stopped there, he wrote to Musa ibn Nusayr informing him of the conquest of Andalus, and of the spoils which he had found. Musa then wrote to [the caliph] Walid Abd al Malik informing him of that, and throwing himself upon his mercy. Musa wrote to Tariq ordering him not to leave Cordoba until he should come to him. And he reprimanded him very severely. Afterwards Musa ibn Nusayr set out for Andalus, in Rajab of the year 93, taking with him the chiefs of the Arabs, the commanders, and the leaders of the Berbers to Andalus. He set out being angry with Tariq, and took with him Habib ibn Abi Ubaida Al Fihri, and left the government of Qairouan to his son Abdallah who was his eldest son. He then passed through Alchadra, and afterwards went over to Cordoba. Tariq then met him, and tried to satisfy him, saying: 'I am merely thy slave, this conquest is thine.' Musa collected of the money a sum, which exceeded all description. Tariq delivered to him all that he had plundered.

Source: Ibn Abd al Hakam, *History of the Conquest of Spain*, translated by John Harris Jones (1858), pp. 18–22. Text updated.

Appendix
5. Bishop John of Nikiu on the conquest of Egypt,
seventh century


John of Nikiu is an important non-Muslim source on the Arab
conquest of Egypt. John was a seventh-century Coptic bishop
whose chronicle includes extensive detail about the Arab
invasion. Here he makes clear the internal dissension prevailing
within Egypt on the eve of the conquests and his own dislike
for the conquerors' creed. He also provides a tantalizing and
controversial hint that 'people began to help the Muslims' during
their invasion and occupation, likely a reference to the Copts.


Moreover, there prevailed great indignation between Theodore the general and the governors owing to the charges
brought by the emperor. And both Theodosius and Anastasius
went forth to the city of On, on horseback, together with a large
body of foot soldiers, in order to attack Amr the son of Al As
(Amr ibn al As). Now the Muslim had not as yet come to know
the city of Misr. And paying no attention to the fortified cities
they came to a place named Tendunias, and embarked on the river. And Amr showed great vigilance and strenuous thought in his
attempts to capture the city of Misr. But he was troubled because
of his separation from (a part of) the Moslem troops, who being
divided into two corps on the east of the river were marching
towards a city named Ain Shams, i.e. On, which was situated on
high ground. And Amr the son of Al As sent a letter to [the ca-
liph] Umar the son of Al Khattab in the province of Palestine to
this effect: 'If thou dost not send Muslim reinforcements, I shall
not be able to take Misr.' And he sent him 4,000 Muslim warriors. And their general's name was Walwarja. He was of barbarian

descent. And he divided his troops into three corps. One corps he placed near Tendunias, the second to the north of Babylon in Egypt; and he made his preparations with the third corps near the city of On. And he gave the following orders: 'Be on the watch, so that when the Roman troops come out to attack us, you may rise up in their rear, whilst we shall be on their front, and so having got them between us, we shall put them to the sword.' And thus when the Roman troops, unaware (of this design), set out from the fortress to attack the Muslim, these Muslims thereupon fell upon their rear, as they had arranged, and a fierce engagement ensued. And when the Muslims came in great numbers against them, the Roman troops fled and betook themselves to the ships. And the Muslim army took possession of the city of Tendunias; for its garrison had been destroyed, and there survived only 300 soldiers. And these fled and withdrew into the fortress and closed the gates. But when they saw the great slaughter that had taken place, they were seized with panic and fled by ship to Nakius in great grief and sorrow. And when Domentianus of the city of Faiyum heard of these events, he set out by night without informing the inhabitants of (A)buit that he was fleeing to escape the Muslims, and they proceeded to Nakius by ship. And when the Muslims learnt that Domentianus had fled, they marched joyously and seized the cities of Faiyum and (A)buit and they shed much blood there.

...

And after the capture of Faiyum with all its territory by the Muslims, Amr sent Abakiri of the city of Dalas requesting him to bring the ships of Rif in order to transport to the east bank of the river the Ishmaelites who were upon the west. And he mustered all his troops about him in order to carry on a vigorous warfare, and he sent orders to the prefect George to construct for him a bridge on the river of the city Qaljub with a view to the capture of all the cities of Misr, and likewise of Athrib and Kuerdis. And people began to help the Muslims. And (the Muslims) captured the cities of Athrib and Manuf, and all their territories. And he had moreover a great bridge constructed over the river near Babylon in Egypt to prevent the passage of ships to Nakius, Alexandria, and upper Egypt, and to make it possible for horses to cross from the western to the eastern bank of the river. And so they effected the submission of all the province of Misr. But Amr was not satisfied with what he had already done, and so he had the Roman magistrates arrested, and their hands and feet confined in iron and wooden bonds. And he forcibly despoiled (them) of much of (their) possessions, and he doubled the taxes on the peasants and forced them to carry fodder for their horses, and he perpetrated innumerable acts of violence. And such of the governors as were in the city of Nakius fled and betook themselves to the city of Alexandria, leaving Domentianus with a few troops to guard the city. And they sent orders also to Dares the chief officer in the city of Samnud to guard the two rivers. Then a panic fell on all the cities of Egypt, and all their inhabitants took to flight, and made their way to Alexandria, abandoning all their possessions and wealth and cattle.

...

And when those Muslims, accompanied by the Egyptians who had apostatized from the Christian faith and embraced the faith of the beast, had come up, the Muslims took as a booty all the possessions of the Christians who had fled, and they designated the servants of Christ enemies of God. And Amr left a large body of his men in the citadel of Babylon in Egypt, and marched in person towards the two rivers in the direction of the east against the general Theodore.

Source: *The Chronicle of John, Bishop of Nikiu*, English translation, 1916, pp. 180–183.

Note. Sources 1, 2 and 4 can be found at Fordham University's online site for medieval Islamic sources: https://sourcebooks.fordham.edu/sbook1d. asp. Al Tabari's volume on the conquest of Iraq is available at https:// www.muslim-library.com/english/the-history-of-al-tabari-vol-13-the- conquest-of-iraq-southwestern-persia-and-egypt/ and John of Nikiu's chronicle at https://archive.org/details/JohnOfNikiuChronicle1916/page/ n199/mode/2up.

# Acknowledgements

My sincere thanks first of all to my agent Georgina Capel for helping turn an idea into this book. At Head of Zeus I am extremely grateful to Anthony Cheetham, to my editor Richard Milbank and to Ben Prior, Jessie Price, Anna Nightingale, Isambard Thomas, Clémence Jacquinet, and Jamie Whyte. Thank you also to Jill Sawyer for her excellent close work on the text.

This is a small book that aims to cover a vast and unwieldy field. In order to make this possible, and in the spirit of the Arab Conquests, I have therefore raided earlier histories and plundered mercilessly. No blood has been spilled in the writing of this book.

# Notes

## 1 INTRODUCTION

1 Cited in Hugh Kennedy, *The Great Arab Conquests: How the Spread of Islam Changed the World We Live In*, p. 41.

2 Abolqasem Ferdowsi, *Shahnameh: the Persian Book of Kings*, p. 847.

3 F. E. Peters, *Jerusalem: The Holy City in the Eyes of Chroniclers, Visitors, Pilgrims, and Prophets from the Days of Abraham to the Beginnings of Modern Times*, p. 175.

4 Karen Armstrong, *A History of God*, p. 203.

5 Tim Mackintosh-Smith, *Arabs: A 3,000-Year History of Peoples, Tribes and Empires*, p. 44.

## 2 MOHAMMED AND THE ROAD TO CONQUEST

6 Cited in Francis E. Peters, *Mecca: A Literary History of the Muslim Holy Land*, p. 21; *Quran*, 14:37; H. Lammens, 'Mecca', *Encyclopedia of Islam*, Vol. 5, p. 439.

7 Ibn Ishaq, *The Life of Muhammad*, p. 464.

8 *Quran*, 8:1; 48:20; 8:69.

9 Patricia Crone, *Meccan Trade and the Rise of Islam*, p. 244.

10 Ibid., p. 547.

11 Peters, Ibid., p. 89.

## 3 INTO THE HOLY LAND: SYRIA & PALESTINE

12 The *Quran* roundly rejects this trio of pagan goddesses: 'They are but names which you and your fathers have invented: God has vested no authority in them.' (53:23)

13 Philip Hitti, *The Origins of the Islamic State. Being a translation from the Arabic, accompanied with annotations, geographic and historic notes of the Kitab Futuh al-Buldan of al-Imaam abu-l 'Abbas Ahmad ibn Jabir al-Baladhuri*, p. 165.

14 Ibid., p. 167.

15 Hugh Kennedy, *The Great Arab Conquests: How the Spread of Islam Changed The World We Live In*, p. 73.

16 The Council of Chalcedon in 451 asserted the church's official doctrine of the duality of Christ and rejected as heresy the Monophysite doctrine that Christ had only one nature. Henceforth this was the official creed of the Roman Empire.

17 Cited in Walter E. Kaegi, *Byzantium and the Early Islamic Conquests*, p. 65.

18  Hitti, p. 187.

19  N. Elisséeff, 'Dimashq', *Encyclopedia of Islam 2 (EI2)*, Vol. 2, p. 280.

20  Ross Burns, *Damascus: A History*, p. 103.

21  Cited in Robert G. Hoyland, *In God's Path: The Arab Conquests and The Creation of an Islamic Empire*, p. 47.

22  Ibid., p. 45; See also S. D. Goitein and O. Grabar, 'Jerusalem' in C. Edmund Bosworth (ed.), *Historic Cities of the Islamic World*, p. 226.

23  The most accessible English translation of this Stakhanovite historian runs into a head-spinning thirty-nine volumes, or around 10,000 pages.

24  Tabari, *The History of Al Tabari, Vol. 12: The Battle of al-Qadisiyyah and the Conquest of Syria and Palestine*, pp. 191–2.

25  Cited in André Raymond, Cairo, pp. 29–30.

26  R. H. Charles (tr.), *The Chronicle of John, Bishop of Nikiu*, pp. 181–2.

27  Cited in Alfred J. Butler, *The Arab Conquest of Egypt and The Last Thirty Years of Roman Dominion*, pp. 269–70.

28  Tabari, *The History of Al Tabari, Vol. 13: The Conquest of Iraq, Southwestern Persia, and Egypt: The Middle Years of Umar's Caliphate*, pp. 170–1.

29  For the fall of Alexandria, see Charles, p. 193.

30  Samir al Khalil [Kanan Makiya], *The Monument: Art, Vulgarity and Responsibility in Iraq*, pp. 1–4.

31  The word 'Iraq' is thought to trace its earliest origins to the Sumerian city of Uruk, dating back to around 4,000 BC, via the Aramaic Erech and possibly Persian Eragh. 'The name *al-Iraq*, for all its Arabic appearance, is derived from Middle Persian *eragh* "lowlands"', says *The Cambridge History of Iran*. Lower Mesopotamia, as the Ancient Greeks referred to the Land between the Rivers, has been called Iraq – from the Arabic for vein or root – since ancient times.

32  For a taste of these hugely absorbing diplomatic exchanges, see Tabari, *The History of al-Tabari, Vol. XII: The Battle of al-Qadisiyyah and the Conquest of Syria and Palestine*, pp. 31–2; 67–73.

33  Abolqasem Ferdowsi, *Shahnameh: Persian Book of Kings*, p. 538.

34  Baladhuri, *The Origins of the Islamic State*, p. 383.

35  'It was wonderfully interesting showing that splendid place to Faisal [King of Iraq],' Gertrude Bell, the British writer, explorer, sometime official and kingmaker, wrote of a visit to Ctesiphon on 2 August 1921. 'He is an inspiring tourist. After we had reconstructed the palace and seen Khosroes [Khosrow] sitting in it, I took him to the high windows to the South, when we could see the Tigris, and told him the story of the Arab conquest as Tabari records it, the

fording of the river and the rest of the magnificent tale. It was the tale of his own people. You can imagine what it was like reciting it to him. I don't know which of us was the more thrilled.' Gertrude Bell, *Letters, Vol. 2* (1927).

36   Tabari, *The History of al-Tabari, Vol. XIII: The Conquest of Iraq, Southwestern Persia, and Egypt*, p. 25.

37   Ibid., p. 28.

38   Ashurbanipal, a king-slaying, lion-hunting warrior, scholar and empire-builder, was not backwards in coming forwards. He left a fantastically boastful account of his conquest on a cuneiform tablet: 'Susa, the great holy city, abode of their gods, seat of their mysteries, I conquered. I entered its palaces, I opened their treasuries where silver and gold, goods and wealth were amassed… I destroyed the ziggurat of Susa. I smashed its shining copper horns. I reduced the temples of Elam to naught; their gods and goddesses I scattered to the winds. The tombs of their ancient and recent kings I devastated, I exposed to the sun, and I carried away their bones toward the land of Ashur. I devastated the provinces of Elam and, on their lands, I sowed salt.'

39   Ibid., pp. 145–6.

40   *Khuzistan Chronicle*. For a discussion of the episode, see Chase Robinson, *The conquest of Khuzistan: a historiographical reassessment*, p. 18.

41   Tabari, Ibid., p. 183.

42   Abd al-Husain Zarrinkub, 'The Arab conquest of Iran and its aftermath' in *The Cambridge History of Iran, Vol. 4: From the Arab Invasion to the Saljuqs*, p. 17; Parvaneh Pourshariati, *Decline and Fall of the Sasanian Empire: The Sasanian-Parthian Confederacy and the Arab Conquest of Iran*, p.257.

43   Tabari, *The History of al-Tabari, Vol. XV: The Crisis of the Early Caliphate*, p. 90.

44   Ferdowsi, *Shahnameh*, p. 957.

6   WE NEED TO TALK ABOUT MUAWIYA

45   Tabari, *The History of al-Tabari, Vol. 15: The Crisis of the Early Caliphate*, p. 11.

46   'The people kept on coming and crying over it as it hung on the pulpit, with the fingers attached to it, for a whole year. The Syrian soldiers swore an oath that they would not make love to women or perform the major ritual ablution unless obligated by seminal discharge during sleep or sleep on beds until they had killed the killers of Uthman and anyone who might block their path in any way, unless they should die meanwhile. They remained around the shirt for a year. It was placed each day on the pulpit, sometimes it was made to cover it and was draped over it, and Naila's fingers were attached to its cuffs.' Tabari, *The History of al-Tabari, Vol. XVI: The Community Divided*, pp. 196–7.

47   Cited in Wilferd Madelung, *The Succession to Muhammad: A Study of the Early Caliphate*, p. 334.

48  Roy Mottahedeh, 'The Abbasid Caliphate in Iran', in *The Cambridge History of Iran, vol. IV: The Period from the Arab Invasion to the Saljuqs*, p. 57; Al Makrizi, *Book of Contention and Strife Concerning the Relations between the Banu Umayya and the Banu Hashim*, p. 92; Gerard Degeorge, *Damascus*, p. 43.

49  In his landmark study, *The Succession to Muhammad: A Study of the Early Caliphate*, Wilferd Madelung refers to Muawiya as a 'brute' with 'a taste for despotism', a 'limited and primitive' judgement of human nature and a predilection for 'bribing, cheating, extorting, intimidating and murdering his way through his reign'.

50  Ross Burns, *Damascus: A History*, p. 124.

51  Cited in Hugh Kennedy, *The Great Arab Conquests: How the Spread of Islam Changed The World We Live In*, p. 210.

52  See Firas Alkhateeb, *Lost Islamic History: Reclaiming Muslim Civilisation from the Past*, p. 51.

53  The absence of such a state gives the lie to the modern jihadist obsession with the 'perfect' caliphate, which exists more in their imagination than in historical reality.

54  R. Stephen Humphreys, *Mu'awiya ibn Abi Sufyan: From Arabia to Empire*, p. 97.

55  Cited in Gerard Degeorge, *Damascus*, p. 31.

56  Humphreys, p. 103.

57  Robert Hoyland, *In God's Path: The Arab Conquests*, pp. 228–9.

58  Saint John of Damascus, *The Fount of Knowledge* in *The Fathers of the Church, Vol. XXXVII*, p. 153.

59  Yaqubi, *Tarikh ibn Wadih* (1883), Vol. 2, p. 283. Cited in Philip Hitti, *Capital Cities of Arab Islam*, p. 68.

7    FROM THE ROOF OF THE WORLD
     TO THE ENDS OF THE EARTH

60  Ibn Battuta, *The Travels of Ibn Battuta*, p. 99.

61  Sharaf al din Ali Yazdi, *Zafarnama, The History of Timur-Bec, Known by the Name of Tamerlain the Great, Emperor of the Moguls and Tartars: Being an historical Journal of his Conquests in Asia and Europe. Written in Persian by Chereddin Ali, Native of Yezd, his Contemporary. Translated into French by the late Monsieur Petis de la Croix…now faithfully render'd into English [by John Darby]*, Vol. 2, p. 7.

62  Robert G. Hoyland, *In God's Path*, p. 199.

63  Beth K. Dougherty and Edmund A. Ghareeb, *Historical Dictionary of Iraq*, p. 242.

64  Milo Minderbinder is the amoral entrepreneur and war profiteer in Joseph Heller's satire *Catch-22*.

65  See Hugh Kennedy, *The Great Arab Conquests: How the Spread of Islam Changed The World We Live In*, p. 196.

66  Baladhuri, *The Origins of the Islamic State*, p. 301.

67  'Is it not obvious,' asked the Arab geographer Muqaddasi, 'that Abd al Malik, seeing the grandeur and magnificence of the Dome of the Holy Sepulchre, was concerned lest it dazzle the thoughts of the Muslims, and thus he erected above the Rock the Dome now seen there?'

68  Cited in Kennedy, p. 298.

69  See Derryl N. MacLean, *Religion and Society in Arab Sind*, pp. 37–9.

70  Tabari, *The History of al-Tabari, Vol. XXIII: The Zenith of the Marwanid House*, p. 127.

71  A mithqal is equivalent to 4.25g of gold and 4.5g of other commodities.

72  Kennedy, p. 263.

73  E. Bretschneider, *On The Knowledge Possessed by the Ancient Chinese of the Arabs and Arabian Colonies: And Other Western Countries, Mentioned in Chinese Books*, p. 8.

74  Guadalquivir, from the Arabic *Wadi al Kabir*, the Great River.

75  'Chronicle of 754', translated from Latin by Kenneth B. Wolf, in Olivia Remie Constable and Damian Zurro (eds), *Medieval Iberia: Readings from Christian, Muslim, and Jewish Sources*, pp. 34–5.

76  Kenneth Baxter Wolf, *Conquerors and Chroniclers of Early Medieval Spain*, p. 145; Edward Gibbon, *The History of the Decline and Fall of the Roman Empire* (1821), Vol. 6, p. 470.

**8    CONCLUSION**

77  Hoyland, *In God's Path*, p. 134.

78  Abul Faraj al Isfahani, *Kitab al Aghani, Book of Song*, vi.126. Cited in Robert Hamilton, *Walid and his Friends: An Umayyad Tragedy*, p.20.

79  See Chase Robinson, 'The Violence of the Abbasid Revolution' in Yasir Suleiman (ed.), *Living Islamic History: Studies in Honour of Professor Carole Hillenbrand*, p. 236.

80  Just one Umayyad prince, the nineteen-year-old Abd al Rahman, managed to escape the carnage. Evading multiple would-be assassins, who harried him for much of his marathon, five-year flight, he travelled through Palestine, Egypt and right across North Africa to found the Umayyad emirate of Cordoba in the Iberian Peninsula.

81  Hoyland, p. 137.

82  Shia Muslims may also add the words *Aliyan waliyu Allah*, Ali is the viceregent of God.

83  See Fred M. Donner, 'The Islamic Conquests' in Youssef M. Choueiri (ed.), *A Companion to the History of the Middle East*, pp. 46–7.

84  Tim Mackintosh-Smith, *Arabs: A 3,000-Year History of Peoples, Tribes and Empires*, p. xvii.

# Bibliography

Alkhateeb, Firas, *Lost Islamic History: Reclaiming Muslim Civilisation from the Past* (London, 2017)

Antrim, Zayde, *Routes and Realms: The Power of Place in the Early Islamic World* (Oxford, 2012)

Ibn Arabshah, Ahmed, *Tamerlane or Timur the Great Amir*, translated by J. H. Sanders from the Arabic Life by Ahmed ibn Arabshah (London, 1936)

Armstrong, Karen, *A History of God: From Abraham to the Present: The 4,000-year Quest for God* (London, 1999)

— *Muhammad: A Prophet for Our Time* (New York, 2006)

Axworthy, Michael, *Iran: Empire of the Mind: A History from Zoroaster to the Present Day* (London, 2008)

Ibn Battuta, *The Travels of Ibn Battuta* (New York, 2009)

Bennison, Amira, *The Great Caliphs: The Golden Age of the Abbasid Empire* (London, 2009)

Bosworth, C. Edmund, (ed.), *Historic Cities of the Islamic World* (Leiden, 2007)

Bowersock, Glen, *Crucible of Islam* (Cambridge, Massachusetts, 2017)

Burns, Ross, *Damascus: A History* (London, 2005)

Butler, Alfred J., *The Arab Conquest of Egypt and The Last Thirty Years of Roman Dominion* (Oxford, 1902)

*The Cambridge History of Central Asia* (Cambridge, 1990)

*The Cambridge History of Iran, Volume 4: The Period from the Arab Invasion to the Saljuqs* (Cambridge, 1975)

*The New Cambridge History of Islam* (Cambridge, 2010)

Charles, R. H. (tr.), *The Chronicle of John, Bishop of Nikiu* (Merchantville, New Jersey, 2007)

Crone, Patricia, *Meccan Trade and the Rise of Islam* (Princeton, 1987)

— *From Arabian Tribes to Islamic Empire* (Aldershot, 2008)

Degeorge, Gérard, *Damascus* (Paris, 2004)

Donner, Fred M., *The Early Islamic Conquests* (Princeton, 1981)

— *Muhammad and the Believers* (Cambridge, Massachusetts, 2010)

— 'The Historical Context', *The Cambridge Companion to the Quran* (Cambridge, 2006)

*Encyclopedia Islamica* (Leiden, 2008)

Ferdowsi, Abolqasem, *Shahnameh: the Persian Book of Kings* (New York, 2016)

Gibb H. A. R., *The Arab Conquests in Central Asia* (London, 1923)

Glubb, John Bagot, *The Great Arab Conquests* (London, 1980)

Hawting, G., *The Idea of Idolatry and the Emergence of Islam: From Polemic to History* (Cambridge, 1999)

— *The First Dynasty of Islam: The Umayyad Caliphate AD 661–750* (London, 1986)

Hitti, P. K., *History of the Arabs* (New York, 1937)

— (tr.) *The Origins of the Islamic State. Being a translation from the Arabic, accompanied with annotations, geographic and historic notes of the Kitab Futuh al-Buldan of al-Imaam abu-l 'Abbas Ahmad ibn Jabir al-Balladur* (New York, 1916)

— *Capital Cities of Arab Islam* (Minneapolis, 1973)

Hourani, Albert, *A History of the Arab Peoples* (London, 2013)

Hoyland, Robert G., *In God's Path: The Arab Conquests and The Creation of an Islamic Empire* (Oxford, 2015)

— *Seeing Islam as Others Saw It* (Princeton, 1997)

Humphreys, R. Stephen, *Mu'awiya ibn Abi Sufyan: From Arabia to Empire* (Oxford, 2006)

Ibn Ishaq, *The Life of Muhammad*, translated by A. Guillaume (London, 1955)

Kaegi, Walter E., *Byzantium and the Early Islamic Conquests* (Cambridge, 2008)

Kennedy, Hugh, *The Great Arab Conquests: How the Spread of Islam Changed the World We Live In* (London, 2008)

— *Armies of the Caliphs* (London, 2001)

— *The Byzantine and Early Islamic Near East* (Aldershot, 2006)

— *When Baghdad Ruled the Muslim World: The Rise and Fall of Islam's Greatest Dynasty* (Cambridge, Massachusetts, 2005)

Ibn Khaldun, *The Muqaddimah: An Introduction to History* (London, 1978)

Khalek, Nancy, *Damascus after the Muslim conquest* (New York, Oxford, 2011)

al Khalili, Jim, *Pathfinders: The Golden Age of Arabic Science* (London, 2010)

Lyons, Jonathan, *The House of Wisdom: How the Arabs Transformed Western Civilisation* (London, 2008)

Mackintosh-Smith, Tim, *Arabs: A 3,000–Year History of Peoples, Tribes and Empires* (Yale, 2019)

Mango, Cyril, *The Oxford History of Byzantium* (Oxford, 2002)

Marozzi, Justin, *Islamic Empires: Fifteen Cities That Define a Civilization* (London, 2019)

Madelung, Wilferd, *The Succession to Muhammad: A Study of the Early Caliphate* (Cambridge, 1996)

Nicolle, David, *The Great Islamic Conquests* (Oxford, 2009)

Peters, F. E., *Jerusalem: The Holy City in the Eyes of Chroniclers, Visitors, Pilgrims, and Prophets from the Days of Abraham to the Beginnings of Modern Times* (Princeton, 1985)

— *Mecca: A Literary History of the Muslim Holy Land* (Princeton, 2017)

— *Muhammad and the Origins of Islam* (Albany, New York, 1994)

Raymond, André, *Cairo* (London, 2000)

Robinson, Chase, *Islamic Historiography* (Cambridge, 2003)

Spuler, Bertold, *The Muslim World. Vol. 1, The Age of the Caliphs* (Leiden, 1960)

Tabari, *The History of Al Tabari*, multiple volumes (Albany, New York, 1985–99)

Wasserstein, David, *The Caliphate in the West: An Islamic Political Institution in the Iberian Peninsula* (Oxford, 1993)

Wolf, Kenneth Baxter, *Conquerors and Chroniclers of Early Medieval Spain* (Liverpool, 1999)

# Picture Credits

pp.4–5 Ivan Soto Cobos / Shutterstock; p.14 Detail of the tilework at the Alcazar Royal Palace, Seville © Isambard Thomas; pp.18–19 Norbert Eisele-Hein/imageBROKER/ Shutterstock; p.21 Bibliothèque Nationale de France / Photo 12 / Alamy Stock Photo; pp.26–7 Images & Stories / Alamy Stock Photo; p.31 Zaruba Ondrej / Shutterstock; pp.32–3 Ashraf Amra/APA Images/ZUMA Wire/Alamy Live News; pp.36–7 Hutchinson's History of the Nations, 1915 / Classic Image / Alamy Stock Photo; p.40 Handout / Alamy Stock Photo; p.49 Science History Images / Alamy Stock Photo; p.50 PHAS/Universal Images Group via Getty Images; pp.52–3 National Library, Madrid / Album / Alamy Stock Photo; p.55 CPA Media Pte Ltd / Alamy Stock Photo; p.56 The Metropolitan Museum of Art / Gift of J. Pierpont Morgan, 1917; pp.58–9 robertharding / Alamy Stock Photo; p.66 Lev Glick / Getty Images; pp.68–9 Heritage Art/Heritage Images via Getty Images; pp.76–7 mohamed abdelattif / Shutterstock; pp.82–3 ahmed el-kabbani / Shutterstock; p.95 Shahnama of Firdawsi, 1614. I.O. ISLAMIC 3265, f.602. British Library / Alamy Stock Photo; pp.100–1 Zoonar/Sergey Mayorov / Alamy Stock Photo; p.103 Jean-Philippe Tournut / Getty Images; pp.106–7 Royal Geographical Society via Getty Images; pp.110–11 Roland and Sabrina Michaud / akg-images; p.113 National Library of France; pp.116–17 Tuul and Bruno Morandi / Alamy Stock Photo; p.120 Zeev Radovan, Department of Antiquities and Museums, Israel / Wikimedia Commons; pp.122–3 The Metropolitan Museum of Art / Purchase, Lila Acheson Wallace Gift, 2004; p.127 Biblioteca Nacional, París / Alamy Stock Photo; pp.128–9 Ayhan Altun / Alamy Stock Photo; p.131 Daniele SCHNEIDER / Getty Images; p.132 Amirah Adlina binti Zulkifli / Wikimedia Commons; pp.136–7 akg-images / Erich Lessing; p.139 Al hilali al sulaymi / Wikimedia Commons; pp.142–3 Alexandre Rotenberg / Alamy Stock Photo; pp.152–3 Gift of K. Thomas Elghanayan in honor of Nourollah Elghanayan / Bridgeman Images; p.154 Tekstbureau De Eindredactie / Getty Images; p.157 akg-images / heritage images / Ashmolean Museum; pp.158–9 Soltan Frédéric/Sygma via Getty Images; pp.162–3 Marji Lang / Getty Images; p.165 Kenneth Garrett / Danita Delimont / Alamy Stock Photo; p.166 Tuul & Bruno Morandi / Getty Images; p.169 Mlenny / Getty Images; pp.170–1 Sean Pavone / Shutterstock; pp.174–5 John Turp / Getty Images; pp.176–7 akg-images / Erich Lessing; p.179 Wu Swee Ong / Getty Images; pp.184–5 3rik Albers / Wikimedia Commons; p.187 DEA PICTURE LIBRARY / Getty Images; p.194 Photo 12/Universal Images Group via Getty Images.

# Index

# M

Madain, fall of (637) 208–10
Maghreb 166, 211
Maiuma, Palestine 144
Makshuh, Qais ibn 203
Mamluk architecture 156
Manat 47
Mandaeans 22
Manichaeans 22
Manuf 218
Martina 81
Marwan II, caliph 182, 184, 186–7, 199, 211
Maslama, Habib ibn 122, 124, 197, 203
Masts, Battle of the (655) 124, 197
Maslul, Sayf Allah al 'The Drawn Sword of God' 60
Maurianos 122, 197
Maurice, Emperor 54, 196
Mawarannahr ('What is Beyond the River') 164
Maysum 141
Maysur, Al Rufayl ibn 210
Mazar-e Sharif 150
Mecca 23
  Mohammed and 30–1, 34, 35, 38, 40–1, 42, 47, 54, 65, 121, 196
  Muawiya and 120, 121
  siege of (692) 151, 198
  Third Fitna or civil war and 186, 199
Medina 84, 91, 102, 108, 124
  Mohammed and 34–5, 39, 42, 196
  Muawiya and 135, 140, 141
  Third Fitna or civil war and 186, 199

Wars of Apostasy and 48, 51
Mehmed II, Sultan 137
Mennas 78
Merv 20, 114, 115, 186, 197, 199
Mesopotamia 98, 99, 122, 202
Messner, Reinhold 62
Mihran, General 102, 209
Misr al Fustat (City of the Tents) 74, 84, 197, 211, 216, 217, 218
Mohammed, Al Sari Shuayb Sayf 209–10
Mohammed, Prophet 17, 22, 51, 92, 103, 109, 120, 121, 125, 126, 137, 149, 151, 156
  Aisha (Prophet's widow) 125, 197
  Al Khandaq battle and 38
  Badr battle and 35, 196
  birth 30–1, 196
  Companions of the Prophet and 51, 79, 88, 92, 102, 103, 108, 121, 126, 138
  death 17, 22, 42, 47, 48, 64, 92, 193, 196
  *hadith* (sayings of the Prophet) 108, 189, 191
  *hijra* (migration) 34, 196
  last years devoted to uniting quarrelling tribes of Arabia under the banner of Islam 41–2
  Mecca, conquest of 35, 38, 40–1, 121, 196
  Night Journey 65

Quran and 16, 24, 31, 38, 42, 51, 96, 108, 124, 144, 149, 150, 184, 188–9, 190, 206
Quraysh tribe and 31, 103
Qurayza Jews, slaughter of 38–9
receives first divine revelation 31, 54, 198
Shia and 109, 186
St John of Damascus and 144
Mongols 148
Morocco. 24, 139, 187
Mosul. 40, 105
Muadh, Saad ibn 38
Muawiya (ibn Sufyan), caliph 65, 108, 120–45, 151, 182–3, 187, 196, 197, 198, 202–3
Mugarrin, Amr ibn 209
Mughals 39
Muhajir, Abu al 139
Muhallab, Al 209
Multan 160–1
Muqaddasi 31, 74, 84
Musa, Abd al Aziz ibn 178
Muslim calendar 34
Muslim, Abd al Rahman ibn 167–8, 172, 178
Muslim, Qutayba ibn 165–72, 198
Mutah, Battle of (628) 47

# N

Nadir 35, 196
Naila 125
Najaf 108
Napoleon 84

Nasser, Abdel 189
NATO 148
Nawakiyah bow 97
Nebuchadnezzar 65, 98
Negev Desert 122
Nestorian Church 91, 91*n*,
104, 141
Night Journey 65
Night of Fury/Night of
Howling 96
Nihavand, Battle of (642)
112, 197
Nineveh 196; Battle of (627)
57, 90
Nizak, prince of Badghis
167–8
Nusayr, Musa ibn 172–5, 178,
198, 199, 211–12, 214, 215

# O

Oman 24, 46
Ottomans 39
Oxus, River 137, 164

# P

Pakistan 160
Palestine 20, 30, 48, 60, 66,
70, 75, 120, 121, 122, 144,
202, 205, 216
Pamir mountains 164
Parthian Empire 98
Paykand 166
Peacock Army 155
Pelusium. 78–9
Penkaye, John 141
Persian Empire 22, 57, 90,
148

Persian Gulf (Arabian Gulf)
46, 89, 108
Phocas 54
Phoenicians 124
pilgrimage 42, 144, 188
Punjab 161

# Q

Qadisiyya, Battle of (636)
88–90, 92, 94, 96–8, 109,
114, 196, 208
Qairouan 138, 198, 211–12,
215
Qais, Al Ashaath ibn 203
Qaljub 217
Qara Qum (Black Sands)
desert 165
Qasim, Mohammed ibn al
160, 169, 174
Qasr al Hayr al Sharqi 184
Qasr Amra 184
Qatar 46
Qaynuqa 35, 196
Quran 16, 24, 31, 38, 42, 51,
96, 108, 124, 144, 149, 150,
184, 188–9, 190, 206
Quraysh 31, 34, 35, 38, 40–1,
47, 51, 54, 92, 103, 120, 122,
126, 138
Qurayza 38, 39, 41

# R

Rahal, Khalid al 88
*ramdaa Makka* (burning of
Mecca) 31
Rasal Khaimah 46

Rashidun 'Rightly Guided'
caliphs 39, 108, 126
Ray 165
Rayhana 38
Reconquista (1492) 179, 211
Red Sea 46, 84
Reshtuni, Theodore 124
Rhodes 81, 124, 197
Rhône valley 178, 199
Ribai 92–4
Ridda Wars/Wars of
Apostasy 48, 51, 103, 196
Roderic, King 172, 198, 212,
214
Roman Empire 48, 57, 64, 74,
80, 81, 98, 137, 172, 217, 218
Rufayl, Sari Shuayb Sayf al
Nadr ibn al Sari ibn al
210

# S

Saad, Laith ibn 214
Sabratha 137
Saffa, caliph Al 'Shedder of
Blood' 130, 135, 186, 199
Sajjah 48
Samarkand 24, 39, 105, 137,
161, 164, 167, 168, 198
Samarra 108
Samnud 218
Sar-o Tar (Place of
Desolation and
Emptiness) 149
Saracens 22, 66
Saragossa 173
Sarjun, Mansur ibn 60
Sasanian Empire of Persia 57
Arab conquests force
disintegration of/